Practice Papers for SQA Exams

Standard Grade | Foundation/General

English

Introduction	3
Topic Index	6
Exam A	
Foundation	7
General	17
Exam B	
Foundation	25
General	33
Exam C	
Foundation	41
General	51
F/G Writing Exam	59
Worked Answers	
Exam A Foundation	69
Exam A General	74
Exam B Foundation	78
Exam B General	82
Exam C Foundation	89
Exam C General	95
F/G Writing Exam	101

ISBN 978-1-84372-785-9

Published by
Leckie & Leckie Ltd, 3rd floor, 4 Queen Street, Edinburgh, EH2 1JE
Tel: 0131 220 6831 Fax: 0131 225 9987
enquiries@leckieandleckie.co.uk   www.leckieandleckie.co.uk

A CIP Catalogue record for this book is available from the British Library.

Leckie & Leckie Ltd is a division of Huveaux plc.

Questions and answers in this book do not emanate from SQA. All of our entirely new and original Practice Papers have been written by experienced authors working directly for the publisher

Text acknowledgements
The following organizations have very generously given permission to reproduce their copyright material free of charge:
The Barn Owl Trust (General Reading exam A),
Extract from 'More Horowitz' (Foundation Reading exam C) by Anthony Horowitz, published by Orchard Books.

Leckie & Leckie is grateful to the copyright holders, as credited below, for permission to use their material:
Extract from 'The Lieutenant' (General Reading exam B) by Kate Grenville, first published in Great Britain by Canongate Books Ltd, 14 High Street, Edinburgh, EH1 1TE
Extract from 'Made in America' (General Reading exam C) by Bill Bryson, published by Black Swan. Reprinted by permission of the Random House Group Ltd.

Every effort has been made to trace the copyright holders and to obtain their permission for the use of copyright material. Leckie & Leckie will gladly receive information enabling them to rectify any error or omission in subsequent editions.

Photograph acknowledgements
All photographs in FG Writing exam © 2009 Jupiterimages Corporation

Introduction

Layout of the Book

This book contains practice exam papers, which mirror the actual SQA exam as much as possible. The layout, paper colour and question level are all similar to the actual exam that you will sit, so that you are familiar with what the exam paper will look like.

The answer section is at the back of the book. Each answer contains a worked-out answer or solution so that you can see how the right answer has been arrived at. The answers also include practical tips on how to tackle certain types of questions, details of how marks are awarded and advice on just what the examiners will be looking for.

Revision advice is provided in this introductory section of the book, so please read on!

How To Use This Book

The Practice Papers can be used in two main ways:

1. You can complete an entire practice paper as preparation for the final exam. If you would like to use the book in this way, you can complete the practice paper under exam-style conditions by setting yourself a time for each paper and answering it as well as possible without using any references or notes.
    Alternatively, you can answer the practice paper questions as a revision exercise, using your notes to produce a model answer. Your teacher may mark these for you.

2. You can use the Topic Index at the front of this book to find all the questions within the book that deal with a specific topic. This allows you to focus specifically on areas that you particularly want to revise or, if you are mid-way through your course, it lets you practise answering exam-style questions for just those topics that you have studied.

Revision Advice

Work out a revision timetable for each week's work in advance – remember to cover all of your subjects and to leave time for homework and breaks. For example:

Day	6pm–6.45pm	7pm–8pm	8.15pm–9pm	9.15pm–10pm
Monday	Homework	Homework	English revision	Chemistry revision
Tuesday	Maths revision	Physics revision	Homework	Free
Wednesday	Geography revision	Modern Studies revision	English revision	French revision
Thursday	Homework	Maths revision	Chemistry revision	Free
Friday	Geography revision	French revision	Free	Free
Saturday	Free	Free	Free	Free
Sunday	Modern Studies revision	Maths revision	Modern Studies revision	Homework

Make sure that you have at least one evening free each week to relax, socialise and re-charge your batteries. It also gives your brain a chance to process the information that you have been feeding it all week.

Arrange your study time into sessions of 30 minutes or 1 hour, with a break between sessions e.g. 6pm–7pm, 7.15pm–7.45pm, 8pm–9pm. Try to start studying as early as possible in the evening when your brain is still alert and be aware that the longer you put off starting, the harder it will be to start!

Study a different subject in each session, except for the day before an exam.

Do something different during your breaks between study sessions – have a cup of tea, or listen to some music. Don't let your 15 minutes expanded into 20 or 25 minutes though!

Have your class notes and any textbooks available for your revision to hand as well as plenty of blank paper, a pen, etc. You may like to make keyword sheets like the geography example below:

Keyword	Meaning
Anticyclone	An area of high pressure
Secondary Industry	Industries that manufacture things
Erosion	The process of wearing down the landscape

Finally forget or ignore all or some of the advice in this section if you are happy with your present way of studying. Everyone revises differently, so find a way that works for you!

Transfer Your Knowledge

As well as using your class notes and textbooks to revise, these practice papers will also be a useful revision tool as they will help you to get used to answering exam-style questions. You may find as you work through the questions that they refer to a case study or an example that you haven't come across before. Don't worry! You should be able to transfer your knowledge of a topic or theme to a new example. The enhanced answer section at the back will demonstrate how to read and interpret the question to identify the topic being examined and how to apply your course knowledge in order to answer the question successfully.

Command Words

In the practice papers and in the exam itself, a number of command words will be used in the questions. These command words are used to show you how you should answer a question – some words indicate that you should write more than others. If you familiarise yourself with these command words, it will help you to structure your answers more effectively.

Command Word	Meaning/Explanation
Analyse	Explain why a writer has written in a certain way.
Argue	State the arguments for or against a case.
Challenge	Question what another person thinks or says.
Comment on	Explain and/or describe
Compare	Give the key features of two different items or ideas and discuss their similarities and/or their differences.
Convey	To put across, to communicate/to tell.
Critically evaluate	Judge the success of a particular text.
Define	Give the meaning of.
Describe	Write in detail about the features of a movement/ action/person/object.
Find evidence	Find quotes from the passage.
Express	Write/explain
Justify	Give reasons for your answer, stating why you have taken an action or reached a particular conclusion.
Suggest	Give an idea or suggestion.
Summarise	Condense into a shortened form.

In the Exam

Watch your time and pace yourself carefully. Work out roughly how much time you can spend on each answer and try to stick to this.

Be clear before the exam what the instructions are likely to be, for example how many questions you should answer in each section. The practice papers will help you to become familiar with the exam's instructions.

Read the question thoroughly before you begin to answer it – make sure you know exactly what the question is asking you to do. If the question is in sections e.g. 15a, 15b, 15c, etc, make sure that you can answer each section before you start writing.

Plan your answer by jotting down keywords, a mindmap or reminders of the important things to include in your answer. Cross them off as you deal with them and check them before you move on to the next question to make sure that you haven't forgotten anything.

Don't repeat yourself as you will not get any more marks for saying the same thing twice. This also applies to annotated diagrams, which will not get you any extra marks if the information is repeated in the written part of your answer.

Give proper explanations. A common error is to give descriptions rather than explanations. If you are asked to explain something, you should be giving reasons. Check your answer to an 'explain' question and make sure that you have used plenty of linking words and phrases such as 'because', 'this means that', 'therefore', 'so', 'so that', 'due to' and 'the reason is'.

Use the resources provided. Some questions will ask you to 'describe and explain' and provide an example or a case study for you to work from. Make sure that you take any relevant data from these resources.

Good luck!

Topic Index

Topic	Foundation Reading Exam A ('Mamo and Tiggist')	General Reading Exam A ('Barn Owl Trust')	Foundation Reading Exam B ('Coming and England')	General Reading Exam B ('The Lieutenant')	Foundation Reading Exam C ('The Hitchhiker')	General Reading Exam C ('Made in America')
Under-standing	2, 3, 4, 5, 7, 9, 10, 11(a) 12, 14(b), 16, 17, 19	1, 3, 4, 6, 7, 8, 10, 11, 12, 16	1, 2, 3, 5, 7	1, 3, 4, 5, 10, 11, 16	2, 3, 7, 9, 17, 16	1, 3, 4, 7
Finding Evidence	1, 8, 11(b), 16	15	4, 6, 15	9, 19	1, 4, 5, 12	7, 9b, 12c
Analysis	6, 13, 14(a), 20	2, 5, 9, 13	14	2, 15	11, 22	2, 11
Evaluation	18, 21	18	18, 19	22	18, 25	17, 18
Word Choice	13, 14(a)	2, 13	8	7	14	6, 14
Imagery	6, 20		10	21	13	9
Sentence Structure		17		12	19	13

Foundation Exam A

English

Standard Grade: Foundation

Practice Papers
For SQA Exams

Foundation Level
Exam A
Reading

Answer all of the questions

Read the following passage and then answer the questions. Remember to use your own words as much as possible.

Mamo and Tiggist

This is an extract from a story about a boy called Mamo and his sister Tiggist, who live in a very poor part of Addis Ababa in Ethiopia. They wake up one morning with difficult decisions to make.

1. There was no light in the shack, none at all, except when the moon was shining. Mamo could see chinks of it then, through the gaps in the corrugated-iron roof.

2. But the moon wasn't out tonight. Mamo shivered, pulled the ragged blanket over his head and huddled against his sister's warm body. Tiggist had been facing away from him, but she turned over to lie on her back, the bare straw mattress rustling as she moved. He knew she was awake. He knew her eyes were open, and that she was staring up into the pitch-darkness.

3. 'What are we going to do?' he said.

4. 'I don't know.'

5. It was a week since their mother had died. Mamo hadn't felt much about it. Ma had been either sick or drunk for as long as he could remember, and he'd kept out of her way if he could, scared of her sudden, violent rages.

6. Tiggist was the person he loved. Years ago, when he was little, she'd staggered around with him on her hip, though she was hardly more than a toddler herself. She'd always looked out for him, saw that he was fed, picked him up when he fell over and screeched at anyone who threatened to hurt him.

7. 'You're not going off, Tiggist, are you?' he said, his stomach suddenly contracting. 'You're not going to leave me?'

8. 'I don't know,' she said again.

9. A black hole seemed to open up in front of Mamo. He wanted to push her, to force her to make promises, but there was a note in his sister's voice that he'd never heard before. It shrivelled him up. His skin was prickling all over.

10. 'The rent's due next week,' she said. 'It's fifty *birr. How are we going to find fifty birr?'

11. Fifty birr! Mamo had never seen so much money in his life.

12. 'What'll they do,' he said, 'if we can't pay?'

13. 'What do you think? They'll throw us out.'

14. 'Where'll we go?'

15. 'Oh shut up, Mamo. How do I know? Work it out for yourself.'

16. The sharpness in her voice shocked him and made him feel worse. He didn't dare speak again.

17. 'I'll go to Mrs Faridah tomorrow,' Tiggist said at last. 'She got me to deliver stuff to her customers last week. She might give me job. I could sleep in her shop.'

18. Mamo swallowed, and moved abruptly away from her.

19. 'I wouldn't go without you, though.'

20. He could hear the uncertainty in her voice, and his fear turned to fury. He rolled right away from her, taking the blanket with him, and clenched his fists.

21. 'Well, what do you want me to do?' She sounded angry herself. 'Work in a bar? Paint my face up and do it with customers round the back? What else is there?'

22. He hadn't thought about it. He'd assumed they'd go on like before, that somehow Tiggist would do what their mother had done, rustle up the money for the rent each month, and scrape together enough every day for something to eat.

23. 'I'll work,' he muttered, 'I'll get a shoe shine kit.'

24. She snorted.

25. 'Who's going to pay for a shoe-shine kit? And how will you get a pitch? You know how those boys fight over them. You wouldn't stand a chance.'

26. He stuffed his fingers into his ears. He couldn't bear to hear any more. Tiggist pulled at the blanked and he rolled back towards her so that it covered them both again. The old straw in the bare mattress beneath them rustled as they moved.

27. 'If we're not careful,' Tiggist said in a voice that was barely more than a whisper, 'we'll end up on the streets.'

* * * * * * *

28. The sun had come up at last, bringing warmth after the cold night, and the smoke from thousands of breakfast fires, all over Addis Ababa, spiralled up into the bright morning air. Mamo pulled at the piece of sharp-edged corrugated iron which formed the door of the shack. It creaked open, and he stepped outside into the narrow lane, blinking in the bright light.

29. He stood uncertainly, watching people hurrying to their day's work. He ignored the crowds of chattering schoolchildren in their bright blue uniforms, who carried piles of crumpled books under their arms. He'd only gone to school for a couple of years, and he'd left for good ages ago when he was eight years old. There'd been no money since then to pay fees. He'd long since forgotten the letters he'd begun to learn there.

30. He was more interested in the adults. There must be someone, among the clerks in their cotton-drill suits, the motherly women off to market, and the young secretaries and shop-girls with their bright knitted sweaters – among all these people there had to be someone who might help him, who would know what to do.

31. Tiggist had been gone at least half an hour by now. She'd washed her face and hands, tidied her hair and tried to scrub some of the stains out of her old skirt. Then she'd gone off to see Mrs Faridah. He could tell watching the stiffness in her back as she walked quickly away from him down the stony lane, that she was stiff with nerves.

32. Usually, Mamo went down to the street corner in the morning. He knew some of the boys that hung around there. They spent the long hours commenting on passers-by, or playing games on a chipped old game board, or begging off anyone well-dressed who walked past. Sometimes he went the other way, to the music shop. He'd sit on the wall outside, drinking in the melodies that poured through the open door, singing along with them under his breath. Today, though, he felt too anxious to go anywhere.

from *The Garbage King* by Elizabeth Laird

birr   the currency in Ethiopia; 50 birr is about £4

Mamo and Tiggist

	Marks

Write your answers in the spaces provided.

Look at Paragraphs 1 and 2.

1. **Write down three** pieces of evidence which show that Mamo and Tiggist live in great poverty.

    1. _____

    2. _____

    3. _____   **2 1 0**

Look at Paragraphs 3 to 8.

2. **Write down an expression** which shows how Mamo reacted to his mother's death.

    _____   **2 ■ 0**

3. What do the details in Paragraph 6 tell you about the relationship between Mamo and Tiggist?

    _____

    _____   **2 ■ 0**

4. **Write down an expression** which shows Mamo is worried.

    _____   **2 ■ 0**

5. **Describe** Tiggist's response to Mamo's questions.

    _____

    _____   **2 1 0**

Look at Paragraphs 9 to 16.

6. 'A black hole seemed to open up in front of Mamo.' (Paragraph 9)

    What does this tell you about the way Mamo is feeling?

    _____

    _____   **2 ■ 0**

			Marks		

7. 'It shrivelled him up. His skin was prickling all over.'

What do these sentences tell you about the effect Tiggist's voice had on Mamo.

_____

_____   2 1 0

8. Tiggist is very impatient with Mamo.

Write down two ways this is made clear.

1. _____

2. _____   2 1 0

9. Why did Mamo not speak again?

_____

_____   2 ■ 0

Look at Paragraphs 17 to 22.

10. Why did Mamo move away from Tiggist?

_____

_____   2 ■ 0

11. (*a*) Why did Mamo's fear turn to fury?

_____

_____   2 1 0

(*b*) **Write down three** pieces of evidence that show how angry he is with her.

1. _____

2. _____

3. _____   2 ■ 0

12. (*a*) **Write down one word** which shows Mamo had not thought carefully about. the situation.

┌─────────────────────────────┐
│   │
│   │
└─────────────────────────────┘   2 ■ 0

(b) **Write down two expressions** which show they have always been short of money.

1. _____

2. _____   2 1 0

Look at Paragraphs 23 to 27.

13. What does 'muttered' suggest about how Mamo is feeling?

_____

_____   2 ■ 0

14. (a) 'She snorted.'

What does this tell you about Tiggist's attitude to Mamo's plan?

_____

_____   2 1 0

(b) Why does she think that he 'won't stand a chance'?

_____

_____   2 1 0

Look at Paragraphs 28 to 30.

15. Write down two details from paragraph 28 which which will make Mamo feel better than he did before.

1. _____

2. _____   2 1 0

16. Why does Mamo no longer go to school?

_____   2 ■ 0

17. Why is Mamo 'more interested in the adults'?

_____

_____   2 ■ 0

Look at Paragraphs 31 to 32.

18. Do you think Mrs Faridah will get a good impression of Tiggist when she arrives?

Yes	
No	

Give **two** reasons from Paragraph 31 to support your answer.

1. _____

2. _____

19. What is the main attraction for Mamo in going to

(i) the street corner: _____

_____

(ii) the music shop: _____

_____

20. (a) 'drinking in the melodies' (Paragraph 32)

What technique is the writer using in this expression? Choose **one** of the following and tick the box:

rhyme	
metaphor	
alliteration	
simile	

(b) What does the expression suggest about Mamo's attitude to music?

_____

_____

Think about the passage as a whole.

21. Do you think things are going to get better or worse for Mamo and Tiggist in the near future? Tick your choice:

Better	
Worse	

Give **two** reasons from the passage to support your answer.

1. _____

_____

2. _____

_____

Marks		
2	1	0
2	1	0
2	■	0
2	1	0
2	1	0

English Standard Grade: General

Practice Papers
For SQA Exams

**General Level
Exam A
Reading**

Answer all of the questions.

Read the following passage and then answer the questions. Remember to use your own words as much as possible.

Scotland's leading educational publishers

The Barn Owl Trust

This passage is taken from the website of a charity called The Barn Owl Trust.

1   The Barn Owl Trust is a small charity working very hard to conserve one of the most beautiful birds on earth. Anyone who has ever watched a Barn Owl hunting at dusk has surely been touched by the experience but sadly these magical birds have become increasingly rare – and the reasons are all man-made. Lack of food due to intensive farming, the loss of roost and nest sites, road mortality, and a host of other factors are to blame.

2   We should remember, however, that the first reliable population estimate was not produced until 1999 and that evidence of the Barn Owl's historical decline in Britain is largely anecdotal. The often-quoted figure of a 70% decline between the 1930s and 1980s comes from the comparison of two unreliable population estimates. It's quite likely that Barn Owl decline started in the mid-1800s as a result of persecution by gamekeepers, egg collectors and the like. The fact is we shall never know to what extent these activities might have affected the Barn Owl population. Indeed they may have only caused the temporary reduction of local population levels.

3   Nevertheless, there is a strong consensus that Barn Owls must have been a lot more common before the mechanisation of farming. Before the late 1800s, when men and horses worked the land, farming was very much less intensive and there can be little doubt that wildlife in general was much more abundant. In particular, small mammals would have been much more common when there were more hedgerows, more marginal grazing land, and pasture was less intensively grazed. Stored cereal crops (in ricks or barns) became so infested with mice and rats that some enlightened farmers encouraged Barn Owls into their buildings via special access holes ('owl windows'). For a species that cannot hunt in rain and suffers high mortality in severe winters, imagine how indoor hunting might have helped survival.

4   In the late 1800s and early 1900s increasing human population levels and the proliferation of farm machines led to increases in the intensity of land management resulting in the loss of Barn Owl habitat. This accelerated during World War II with a drive for Britain to become more self-sufficient. The idea that British farmers had a duty to produce as much human food as possible (which became deeply ingrained during WWII) continued right up to the 1980s. Ask almost any elderly farmer and he'll probably remember seeing 'fluffy white owls' up on the barn wall when he was a lad in the 1930s. The changes in farming practices stimulated by the legacy of WWII, human population expansion, government policies, and consumer pressure for ever-cheaper food, are the main reason behind the Barn Owl's historical decline in Britain.

5   From the mid 1900s onwards, other factors started to work against the Barn Owl population: the proliferation of mouse and rat baits that kill predators as well as rodents; barns being converted into houses; the impact of the trunk road network (started in the 1950s) which now kills thousands of Barn Owls every year.

6   If the population is to expand, it is essential not only that traditional Barn Owl sites continue to be occupied but that the birds' breeding success is improved and that additional young birds disperse to occupy other sites. There are numerous factors that can cause the loss of occupied sites but fortunately most of these can be prevented by the implementation of sensible protection measures. Steps can also be taken to maximise nesting success and this has been a major part of the Barn Owl Trust's work since 1997 when we created a package of measures to be targeted at all known nest sites.

7   Simply contacting nest site owners and highlighting the owls' presence can go a long way towards securing their protection. Where the owner has plans to alter the site we advise on timing and incorporation of the owls' needs (for example making provision for owls in a barn conversion). We explain the owls' sensitivity to irregular disturbance and tolerance of regular activities. Food availability largely controls survival and nesting success so we identify patches of good habitat and explain their importance and advise on the creation of additional foraging areas. To minimise the chances of secondary poisoning we advise on alternative methods of rodent control.

8   As well as advisory work we carry out practical tasks. Very often the owls' nest place is not as safe as it could be – in particular, nests on ledges or in poorly designed nestboxes can result in young falling from the nest prematurely and dying of injury, neglect, or predation. We erect safer (deep) nestboxes. In case anything should happen to the main nest place we make alternative provision with a second nestbox, normally in another nearby building or tree. Steep-sided water troughs close to nests are a particular problem so we make special floats – one for each water tank within 200 metres of the nest to prevent owls from drowning.

9   Although compared to other charities the Barn Owl Trust is still very small, it has an impressive track record and an excellent reputation. It officially 'hatched' on the 30th July 1988 with the arrival of its registered charity number and a donation of £25 from one of its founding Trustees. That was all it had: a number, twenty-five pounds, and a few highly committed and very active volunteers!

10 In the early days effort was concentrated on habitat creation and boosting the number of wild Barn Owls by releasing additional birds from captivity. The Trust soon began highly detailed countywide surveys that highlighted the ongoing loss of occupied sites. This prompted a major research project looking at the effects of barn conversion on local Barn Owl populations, that in turn led to positive changes in Local Authority planning policies. Other projects have led to close working relationships with a wide range of conservation organisations.

11 Despite having a small team of professional staff and being consulted by government, the Barn Owl Trust is still a grass-roots voluntary organisation that prides itself on the sheer amount of practical work it does. Erecting nesting boxes, creating ideal habitats, providing quality care for injured owls, conducting innovative research and thought provoking educational work, organising specialist training for professionals – the Barn Owl Trust leads the field.

Look at Paragraph 1.

	Marks	

1. **Write down the one word** that best describes the work of the Barn Owl Trust.

    `2  ■  0`

2. **Write down two words** that help to create a positive impression of Barn Owls.

    `2  1  0`

3. **Write down one word** that tells us that there are many reasons why Barn Owls are becoming rare.

    `2  ■  0`

Look at Paragraph 2.

4. **Write down a word** used later in the paragraph which means the same as 'anecdotal'.

    `2  ■  0`

5. **Write down three words or expressions** which show that the writer is not certain about the facts.

    (i) _____

    (ii) _____

    (iii) _____

    `2  1  0`

Look at Paragraph 3.

6. Explain **in your own words** the most likely reason for the decline in Barn Owl numbers from the late 1880s onwards.

    _____

    _____

    `2  1  0`

7. (*a*) Why did some farmers encourage Barn Owls into their buildings?

_____

_____ | 2 | 1 | 0

(*b*) Why would this have been good for the Barn Owls?

_____

_____ | 2 | 1 | 0

Look at Paragraph 4.

8. (*a*) **Explain in your own words** why the loss of Barn Owl habitat increased during World War II.

_____

_____ | 2 | 1 | 0

(*b*) **In your own words**, give **one** other reason for the decline in the numbers of Barn Owls.

_____

_____ | 2 | ■ | 0

Look at Paragraph 5.

9. Explain the function **in this paragraph** of:

(*a*) the colon:

_____

_____ | 2 | 1 | 0

(*b*) the semicolons:

_____

_____ | 2 | 1 | 0

Look at Paragraph 6.

10. Tick the appropriate box to show whether the following statements are True, False, or you Can't Tell from the paragraph.

		True	False	Can't Tell
(a)	There are three things that must happen if the Barn Owl population is to get bigger.			
(b)	Using sensible protection measures will stop the loss of occupied sites.			
(c)	The Barn Owl Trust has managed to maximise nesting success.			

	Marks	
2	■	0
2	■	0
2	■	0

Look at Paragraph 7.

11. Which of the following is the best description of the **main topic** of the paragraph? Tick your choice of answer.

contacting site owners	
explaining owls' behaviour	
preventing the poisoning of owls	
giving advice about owls	

2	■	0

Look at Paragraph 8.

12. (a) **In your own words**, give one example of the 'practical tasks' carried out by the Trust.

_____

_____

2	1	0

(b) Explain the difference between 'advisory work' and 'practical tasks'.

_____

_____

2	1	0

Look at Paragraph 9.

13. **Write down two words or expressions** that create a good impression of the Barn Owl Trust.

(i) _____

(ii) _____

2	1	0

14. Why does the writer put inverted commas round the word 'hatched'?

_____

_____ | 2 | 1 | 0 |

Look at Paragraph 10.

15. What evidence is there that the Barn Owl Trust's work has been successful?

_____

_____ | 2 | 1 | 0 |

Look at Paragraph 11.

16. Write down an expression that means the opposite of 'grass roots volunteers'.

_____ | 2 | ■ | 0 |

17. Explain **the effect** of the following features of **sentence structure** in the last sentence of this paragraph.

(*a*) the list: _____

_____ | 2 | 1 | 0 |

(*b*) putting the main idea at the end: _____

_____ | 2 | 1 | 0 |

Think about the passage as a whole.

18. (i) What do you think is the **main purpose** of this piece of writing? Tick your choice.

to inform readers about Barn Owls	
to inform readers about the work of the Barn Owl Trust	

(ii) Justify your choice by referring to more than one part of the passage.

_____

_____

_____ | 2 | 1 | 0 |

English

Standard Grade: Foundation

Answer all of the questions

Read the following passage and then answer the questions. Remember to use your own words as much as possible.

Coming to England

Floella Benjamin, a well known television presenter, was born in Trinidad and moved to England with her family when still a child. In this chapter from her autobiography, Coming to England, Floella describes her new school.

1. Marmie had made arrangements for us to go to a local school and after just ten days of being in England, I was on my way to my first English school.

2. When I arrived at the school, many of the children rushed over and touched me then ran away giggling. I thought they were being nice to me. At that time I didn't realise it was because I was different, a novelty, something to be made a fool of and to be laughed at. The dingy Victorian building squatted in the large grey playground like a bulldog ready to attack. It was surrounded by high wire fencing, a hopscotch game was marked out on the ground and on one of the walls a bull's-eye pattern was painted.

3. Above the school's main door were some letters engraved in the stone; they were Latin words and I never did find out what they meant. Inside the school the walls of the long corridors were tiled halfway up, making the building feel cold. The tiles had been painted a mushy green, some of it flaking off where it had been scratched over the years by passing children. The ceilings and upper half of the walls were a dull beige colour and the floors were covered with worn and splintering wooden parquet*. Off the corridors were separate, unwelcoming classrooms, each one with its own door, not partitions like the ones in Trinidad. But the desks and the blackboards were the same. I felt a little comforted when I saw them. At least they were something I'd seen before.

4. The structure of the day was also a familiar routine: lessons, playtime, more lessons, lunch and play, then ending the day with more lessons. The work the teacher gave us was so easy and simple compared to the work I was used to. Yet the teacher treated me like an idiot because she couldn't understand my Trinidadian accent even though I could understand her. I felt like a fish out of water.

5. School took a great deal of getting used to, especially during the first few weeks. I found some things new and exciting – simple things like the taste of cold milk during the morning break. I would grip the small glass bottle tightly as I plunged the straw into the silver foil top and sucked out the creamy liquid. The only thing I wasn't so keen on was the thick, furry feeling it left in my mouth afterwards. There wasn't a stall selling treats in the playground but the children did play clapping and skipping games which made me feel at home. There was one game, however, which I didn't understand at first but in no time at all I began to hate. The first time I saw the children play it, I knew that it was wrong and cruel. I was standing next to the wall with the painted bull's eye when some boys came up to me and spat strange words at me, words that I had never heard before but from their faces I knew that they were not nice. They were words which told me that I was different from them and that they felt my kind shouldn't be in their country. I looked at them, confused and baffled like a trapped, helpless creature. What was 'my kind' and why shouldn't I be in the country I was brought up to

love? The land of hope and glory, mother of the free. I began to feel angry and violent as I stood and watched their ugly faces jeering at me. But they might as well have been talking in a foreign language because I didn't understand the words they were shouting. I didn't let them make me cry though, I had learnt how to be tough during the time Marmie had left us in Trinidad. When I got home and asked Marmie what the words meant, she looked sad and sat us all down and slowly explained that because of the colour of our skin some people were going to be cruel and nasty to us. But we must be strong, make something of ourselves and never let them get the better of us. That was the day I realised that in the eyes of some people in this world I was not a person but a colour.

parquet   floorboards

Read Paragraph 1 & 2

	Marks		

1. Who made the arrangements about Floella's school and how long had Floella been in England before she started school?

   [blank box]   [blank box]

   2 1 0

2. What did many of the children do when they first saw Floella?

   _____

   _____

   2 1 0

3. Why did Floella think the children were paying attention to her and what was the real reason?

   _____

   _____

   2 1 0

4. Had the children ever seen someone with a different skin colour before? Quote a word from paragraph 2 to support your answer.

   _____

   _____

   [blank box]

   2 1 0

5. Read again the description of the outside of the school in paragraph 2.

   Tick the appropriate box to show whether the following statements are true, false or cannot be answered from the passage.

	True	False	Cannot tell			
The school was partly enclosed by high wire fencing				2	■	0
Children had marked out a hopscotch game				2	■	0
A bull's eye pattern was painted on one of the walls				2	■	0
There were letters engraved above the main door				2	■	0

6. Read again the description of the inside of the school in paragraph 3.
   Write down three pieces of evidence which tell you the school is not comfortable or newly decorated.

   _____

   _____

   _____

   2 1 0

	Marks	

7. Read paragraph four Name ONE difference and ONE similarity between Floella's school in Trinidad and her school in England.

   Difference _____

   Similarity _____

   | 2 | 1 | 0 |

8. Floella tells us that the structure of the day was 'a familiar routine'. Explain in your own words what this phrase tells you.

   _____

   _____

   | 2 | 1 | 0 |

9. Why did the teacher treat Floella 'like an idiot' and why was this surprising?

   _____

   _____

   | 2 | 1 | 0 |

10. 'I felt like a fish out of water' (paragraph 4). What technique has Floella used here? Explain in your own words what this tells us about how she felt.

    _____

    _____

    | 2 | 1 | 0 |

11. (a) Read paragraph 5 again. Name three things which Floella found 'new and exciting' about drinking milk at school.

    _____

    _____

    _____

    | 2 | 1 | 0 |

    (b) What did Floella not like about drinking milk?

    _____

    | 2 | ■ | 0 |

12. Explain in your own words how Floella felt in paragraph 5 when the children played clapping and skipping games.

    _____

    _____

    | 2 | ■ | 0 |

13. Floella describes a game some boys played which she thought was 'wrong and cruel'.

    (*a*) Explain FULLY what happened in the game

_____

_____

    | 2 | 1 | 0 |

    (*b*) In your opinion, is 'game' is an appropriate word for what the boys did? Answer fully.

_____

_____

    | 2 | 1 | 0 |

14. Why are inverted commas used round the phrase 'my kind'?

_____

_____

    | 2 | ■ | 0 |

15. Floella's feelings towards the boys change.

    (*a*) Quote a phrase in paragraph 5 which tells you how she felt at first during the boys' game.

_____

    | 2 | ■ | 0 |

    (*b*) Quote a phrase in paragraph 5 which tells you how she felt later on during the boys' game.

_____

    | 2 | ■ | 0 |

16. Marmie was the first member of the family to move to England. Why do you think Floella had 'learnt how to be tough' (paragraph 5) during this time?

_____

_____

    | 2 | 1 | 0 |

17. Write down two pieces of advice Marmie gives the children about how to behave when people were 'cruel and nasty'.

_____

_____

    | 2 | 1 | 0 |

Marks

	Marks	

18. 'I was not a person but a colour.' Why do you think Floella has chosen to <u>end</u> her writing with this sentence?

_____

_____

2 1 0

Think about the passage as a whole.

19. The title of this chapter is 'Settling In'. Do you think this is a good title for this chapter and why?

_____

_____

2 1 0

English   Standard Grade: General

Answer all of the questions.

Read the following passage and then answer the questions. Remember to use your own words as much as possible.

Scotland's leading educational publishers

The Lieutenant

In the opening chapter of Kate Grenville's novel 'The Lieutenant', the author describes Daniel Rooke's early schooldays.

1 Daniel Rooke was quiet, moody, a man of few words. He had no memories other than of being an outsider.

2 At the dame school* in Portsmouth they thought him stupid. His first day there was by coincidence his fifth birthday, the third of March 1767. He took his place behind the desk with his mother's breakfast oatmeal cosy in his stomach and his new jacket on, happy to be joining the world beyond his home. Mrs Bartholomew showed him a badly executed engraving with the word 'cat' underneath. His mother had taught him his letters and he had been reading for a year. He could not work out what Mrs Bartholomew wanted. He sat at his desk, mouth open.

3 That was the first time he was paddled* with Mrs Bartholomew's old hairbrush for failing to respond to a question so simple he had not thought to answer it.

4 He could not become interested in the multiplication tables. While the others chanted through them, impatient for the morning break, he was looking under the desk at the notebook in which he was collecting his special numbers, the ones that could not be divided by any number but themselves and one. Like him, they were solitaries*.

5 When Mrs Bartholomew pounced on him one day and seized the notebook, he was afraid she would throw it in the fire and smack him with the hairbrush again. She looked at it for a long time and put it away in her pinny* pocket.

6 He wanted to ask for it back. Not for the numbers, they were in his head, but for the notebook, too precious to lose.

7 Then Dr Adair from the Academy came to the house in Church Street. Rooke could not guess who Dr Adair was, or what he was doing in their parlour*. He only knew that he had been washed and combed for a visitor, that his infant sisters had been sent next door to the neighbour woman, and that his mother and father were sitting on the uncomfortable chairs in the corner with rigid faces.

8 Dr Adair leaned forward. Did Master Rooke know of numbers that could be divided by nothing but themselves and one? Rooke forgot to be in awe. He ran up to his attic room and came back with the grid he had drawn, ten by ten, the first hundred numbers with these special ones done in red ink: two, three, five and on to ninety-seven. He pointed, there was a kind of pattern, do you see, here and here? But one hundred numbers was not enough, he needed a bigger sheet of paper so he could make a square twenty or even thirty a side, and then he could find the true pattern, and perhaps Dr Adair might be able to provide him with such a sheet?

9   His father by now had the rictus* of a smile that meant his son was exposing his oddness to a stranger, and his mother was looking down into her lap. Rooke folded the grid and hid it under his hand on the table.

10   But Dr Adair lifted his fingers from the grubby paper. 'May I borrow this?' he asked. 'I would like, if I may, to show it to a gentleman of my acquaintance who will be interested that it was created by a boy of seven.'

11   After Dr Adair went, the neighbour woman brought his sisters back. She inspected Rooke and said loudly, as if he were deaf, or a dog, 'Yes, he looks clever, don't he?' Rooke felt the hairs on his head standing up with the heat of his blush. Whether it was because he was stupid or clever, it added up to the same thing: the misery of being out of step with the world.

12   When he turned eight Dr Adair offered the bursary*. It was just words: *a place at the Portsmouth Naval Academy*. The boy thought it could not be too different from the life he knew, went along blithely and hardly waved goodbye to his father at the gate. The first night there he lay rigid in the dark, too shocked to cry.

13   The other boys established that his father was a clerk who went every day to the squat stone building near the docks where the Office of Ordnance ran its affairs. In the world of Church Street, Benjamin Rooke was a man of education and standing, a father to be proud of. At the Portsmouth Naval Academy a mile away, he was an embarrassment. *A clerk! Oh dearie me!* A boy took everything out of his trunk, the shirts and underthings his mother and grandmother had so carefully made, and hurled them through the window into the muddy yard three flights below. A man in a billowing black gown caught Rooke painfully by the ear and hit him with a cane when he tried to say that he had not done it. A big boy sat him up on a high wall out behind the kitchens and poked him with a stick until he was forced to jump down.

14   His ankle still hurt from the fall, but that was not the pain at his heart.

15   His attic in Church Street wrapped its corners and angles around him, the shape of his own odd self. At the Academy, the cold space of the bleak dormitory sucked out his spirit and left a shell behind.

16   Walking from the Academy back to Church Street every Saturday evening to spend Sunday at home was a journey between one world and another that wrenched him out of shape each time. His mother and father were so proud, so warm with pleasure that their clever son had been singled out, that he could not tell them how he felt. His grandmother might have understood, but he could not find the words to tell even her how he had lost himself.

17 When it came time for him to walk back, Anne held his hand with both hers, pulling at him with all her child's weight and crying for him to stay. She was not yet five, but somehow knew that he longed to remain anchored in the hallway. His father peeled her fingers away one by one and shooed him out the door, waving and smiling, so that Rooke had to wave too and put a grin on his face. All the way up the street he could hear Anne wailing, and his nan trying to comfort her.

dame school	a type of private primary school run by women
paddled	to be spanked or beaten with a small bat
solitaries	used here to mean prime numbers, i.e. numbers that can only be divided by themselves and one
pinny	shortened form of 'pinafore', which is an apron or overall for women
parlour	a family sitting room or living room
rictus	fixed, open mouth
bursary	a sum of money given to a pupil in financial need to pay for his or her education

Read paragraph 1 again

Marks

1. What did Daniel remember about his childhood?

    _____

    _____

    | 2 | 1 | 0 |

2. Why was 3rd of March 1767 an important date for Daniel?

    _____

    _____

    | 2 | 1 | 0 |

3. In your own words, explain why the teachers at the dame school thought Daniel was 'stupid' (paragraph 2) on his first day at the school.

    _____

    _____

    | 2 | 1 | 0 |

4. Explain in your own words how Mrs Bartholemew reacted to Daniel's silence when she showed him the engraving.

    _____

    _____

    | 2 | ■ | 0 |

5. Explain in your own words why Daniel 'could not become interested in the multiplication tables'? (paragraph 4)

    _____

    _____

    | 2 | 1 | 0 |

6. 'Like him, they were solitaries'. (paragraph 4) What does this expression tell you about Daniel? Refer to the glossary if you need to.

    _____

    _____

    | 2 | 1 | 0 |

7. Explain <u>how</u> Mrs Bartholemew took Daniel's notebook. Quote from paragraph 5 to support your answer.

    _____

    _____

    | 2 | 1 | 0 |

8. Why do you think Mrs Bartholemew (a) 'looked at it for a long time and (b) put it away in her pinny pocket'? (paragraph 5)

    (*a*) _____

    (*b*) _____

    | 2 | 1 | 0 |

	Marks	

9. Did Daniel <u>need</u> or <u>want</u> the book back? Explain your choice, quoting from the passage to support your answer.

_____

_____

2 1 0

10. In what way did the family make an effort to impress Dr Adair? Answer in your own words.

_____

_____

2 1 0

11. How does the writer show that Daniel is not 'in awe' (paragraph 8) of Dr Adair?

_____

_____

2 1 0

12. 'But one hundred numbers … such a sheet.' (paragraph 8) What is unusual about this sentence structure and why has it been used?

_____

_____

2 1 0

13. How did his father feel when Daniel was showing the grid to Dr Adair?

_____

_____

2 ■ 0

14. Why does Dr Adair wish to show Daniel's grid to a friend of his?

_____

_____

2 1 0

Read paragraphs 10 and 11 again.

15. What is the difference between the language Dr Adair uses to speak to Rooke in paragraph 10 and the language the neighbour woman uses to speak to Rooke in paragraph 11?

_____

_____

2 1 0

16. Read paragraph 12 beginning 'When he turned eight.' Explain in your own words how Daniel first felt about attending Portsmouth Naval Academy.

_____

_____

2 1 0

	Marks		

17. *'A clerk! Oh dearie me!'* (Paragraph 13) Suggest who might have spoken these words and why.

_____

_____ **2 1 0**

18. On Daniel's first night at the Academy, he is 'too shocked to cry'. (paragraph 12) Give two examples of things that happened at the Academy on his first day that might have made him shocked.

(*a*) _____

(*b*) _____ **2 1 0**

19. Read paragraph 15 again. Explain in your own words how Daniel felt
    (*a*) at his home in the attic in Church Street

    _____ **2 1 0**

    (*b*) in the dormitory at the Academy

    _____ **2 1 0**

20. Write down an expression in Paragraph 16 which emphasises the contrast between Daniel's home and school.

    _____

    _____ **2 ■ 0**

21. Why did Daniel feel he could not explain his true feelings to his parents?

    _____

    _____ **2 1 0**

22. Daniel's sister Anne knew that Daniel wanted to 'remain anchored in the hallway'. (paragraph 17)

    (*a*) What technique has the writer used here?

    _____ **2 ■ 0**

    (*b*) What does this tell you about how Daniel feels about his home and family?

    _____ **2 ■ 0**

Think about the passage as a whole.

23. This extract comes from the opening of the novel 'The Lieutenant', which tells the story of Daniel's life and search for a sense of 'belonging'. Do you think that this opening is effective in introducing Daniel's life? Answer fully, quoting from the passage to support your answer.

    _____

    _____

    _____

    _____ **2 1 0**

English Standard Grade: Foundation

Practice Papers	**Foundation Level**
For SQA Exams	**Exam C**
	Reading

Answer all of the questions

Read the following passage and then answer the questions. Remember to use your own words as much as possible.

Leckie×Leckie

Scotland's leading educational publishers

The Hitchhiker

In this extract from a short story 'The Hitchhiker' by the writer Anthony Horowitz, a family stops to pick up a hitchhiker on their way home from a day trip.

1. Why did my father have to stop? I told him not to. I knew it was a bad idea. Of course, he didn't listen to me. Parents never do. But it would never have happened if only he'd driven on.

2. We'd been out for the day, just the three of us, and what a great, really happy day it had been. My fifteenth birthday, and they had taken me to Southwold, a small town on the Suffolk coast. We'd got there just in time for lunch and had spent the afternoon walking on the beach, looking in the shops and losing money in the crummy arcade down by the pier.

3. A lot of people would think that Southwold was a rubbish place to go, especially on your birthday. But they'd be wrong. The truth is that it's special. From the multicoloured beach huts that have probably been there since Queen Victoria's time, to the cannons on the cliff which have certainly been there a whole lot longer. It's got a lighthouse and a brewery and a sloping village green that all look as if they've come out of an Enid Blyton story. None of the shops seem to sell anything that anyone would actually want and there's one, in the High Street, that has these fantastic wooden toys. A whole circus that comes to life for twenty pence. And the talking head of Horatio Nelson who puts his telescope up to his missing eye and sings. You get real fish and chips in Southwold. Fish that were still swimming while you were driving to the restaurant. Sticky puddings with custard. I don't need to go on. The whole place is so old-fashioned and so English that it just makes you want to smile.

4. We started back at about five o'clock. There was a real Suffolk sunset that evening. The sky was pink and grey and dark blue and somehow there was almost too much of it. I sat in the back of the car and as the door slammed I felt that strange, heavy feeling you get at the end of a really good day. I was sad that it was over. But I felt happy and tired, glad that it was over too.

5. It was only about an hour's drive and as we left Southwold it began to rain. There's nothing strange about that. The weather often changes rapidly in Suffolk. By the time we reached the A12, the rain was falling quite heavily, slanting down, grey needles in the breeze. And there, ahead of us on the road, was a man, walking quickly, his hands clenched on the sides of his jacket, pulling it around him. He didn't turn round as we approached but he must have heard us coming. Suddenly his hand shot out. One thumb jutted out; the universal symbol of the hitchhiker. He wanted a lift.

6. There were about fifteen seconds until we reached him. My father was the first to speak.

7. 'I wonder where he's going.'
'You're not going to stop,' my mother said.
'Why not? It's a horrible evening. Look at the weather!'

8. And there you have my parents. My father is a dentist and maybe that's why he's always trying to be nice to people. He knows that nobody in their right mind really wants to see him. He's tall and shambolic, the sort of man who goes to work with his hair unbrushed and with socks that don't match. My mother works three days a week at an estate agency. She's much tougher than him. When I was young, she was always the one who would send me to bed. He'd let me stay up all night if she wasn't there.

9. There's one more thing I have to tell you about them. They both look quite a bit older than they actually are. There's a reason for this. My older brother, Eddy. He died suddenly when he was twelve years old. That was nine years ago and my parents have never really recovered. I miss him too. Of course, he bullied me sometimes like all big brothers do, but his death was a terrible thing. It hurt us all and we know that the pain will never go away.

10. Anyway, it was typical of my dad to want to stop and offer the man a lift and just as typical of my mum to want to drive on. In the back seat, I said, 'Don't stop, Dad.' But it was already too late. Just fifteen seconds had passed since we saw the hitchhiker and already we were slowing down. I'd told him not to stop. But I'd no sooner said it than we did.

11. The rain was coming down harder now and it was very dark so I couldn't see very much of the man. He seemed quite large, towering over the car. He had long hair, hanging down over his eyes.

12. My father pressed the button that lowered the window. 'Where are you going?' he asked.
'Ipswich.'

13. Ipswich was about twenty miles away. My mother didn't say anything. I could tell that she was uncomfortable.

14. 'You were heading there on foot?' my father asked.
'My car's broken down.'
'Well – we're heading that way. We can give you a lift.'
'John...' My mother spoke my father's name quietly but already it was too late. The damage was done.
'Thanks,' the man said. He opened the back door.

15. I suppose I'd better explain.

16. The A12 is long, dark anonymous road that often goes through empty countryside with no buildings in sight. It was like that where we were now. There were no street lights. Pulled in on the hard shoulder, we must have been practically invisible to the other traffic rushing past. It was the one place in the world where you'd have to be crazy to pick up a stranger.

17. Because, you see, everyone knows about Fairfields. It's a big, ugly building not far from Woodbridge, surrounded by a wall that's fifteen metres high with spikes along the top and metal gates that open electronically. The name is quite new. It used to be called the East Suffolk Maximum Security Prison for the Criminally Insane. And right now we were only about ten miles away from it.

		Marks		

1. What two phrases in paragraph 1 tells you that the writer of the story did not want his father to stop?

2 1 0

2. Where and why had the family been out for the day?

_____

_____

2 1 0

3. Write down three things the family did in the afternoon.

_____

_____

_____

2 1 0

4. Did the family enjoy the day out? Write down two phrases which tell you this.

2 1 0

5. Write down a word in paragraph 2 which means 'shabby' or 'run-down'

2 ■ 0

6. What might some people think about going to Southwold for a day trip?

_____

_____

2 1 0

7. Read again in paragraph 3 'From the multi coloured beach huts' to 'Enid Blyton story.' Give any two reasons why the boy thinks Southwold is special.

_____

_____

2 1 0

8. The boy describes one of the toys in the toy shop - 'A whole circus that comes to life for twenty pence' (paragraph 3). Explain what this toy might be like.

_____

_____

2 1 0

		Marks	

9. Explain in your own words what the boy means when he says 'I don't need to go on' (paragraph 3)

_____

_____

2	1	0

10. After the car door shut, how did the boy feel? Tick two CONTRASTING words from the list below.

strange	
heavy	
sad	
happy	
tired	
glad	

2	1	0

11. Write down an expression from paragraph 5 which tells you that the writer did not think rain was unusual in Southwold.

2	■	0

12. The writer describes the sunset in paragraph 4 'and somehow there was almost too much of it.' Explain what this phrase means.

_____

_____

2	1	0

13. 'grey needles in the breeze'. What technique is the writer using in this expression? Tick the correct box.

Techniques	Tick
rhyme	
metaphor	
alliteration	
simile	

What does this tell you about the rain?

_____

2	1	0

14. The hitchhiker has his hands 'clenched' (paragraph 5) on the sides of his jacket. Explain what this means in your own words.

_____

_____

| 2 | 1 | 0 |

15. Read again paragraph 8 which describes the writer's father and mother. Who do you think is more likely to want to pick up the hitchhiker? Quote from the passage to support your answer.

_____

_____

| 2 | 1 | 0 |

16. In paragraph 8, the writer's father is described as 'shambolic' which means 'messy'. Write down two examples of how he is messy.

_____

_____

| 2 | 1 | 0 |

17. 'There's one more thing I have to tell you about them' (paragraph 9). What are you told about the child's parents and why do you think the writer tells you this?

_____

_____

| 2 | 1 | 0 |

18. In your opinion, why was the mother 'uncomfortable'? (13)

_____

_____

| 2 | 1 | 0 |

19. 'John...' (paragraph 14). Comment on the structure of this sentence and why it has been used.

_____

_____

| 2 | 1 | 0 |

20. Read again paragraph 16, which begins 'The A12 is a long, dark, anonymous road...' Why do you think it would be 'crazy' (paragraph 16) to pick up a stranger on the A12?

_____

_____

| 2 | 1 | 0 |

	Marks	

21. Write down a word from the same paragraph which means 'nearly'.

2	■	0

22. How does the writer make Fairfields sound an unpleasant place? in paragraph 17

_____

_____

2	1	0

23. Why do you think the name of the prison has been changed from 'East Suffolk Maximum Security Prison for the Criminally Insane' to 'Fairfields'?

_____

_____

2	■	0

Now think about the whole passage.

24. Would you like to visit Southwold? You should refer to ideas from the passage in your answer.

_____

_____

2	1	0

25. Based on what you are told about the hitchhiker in the passage, would you have picked him up? Quote from the passage to support your answer.

_____

_____

2	1	0

Exam C – General Paper

English Standard Grade: General

Practice Papers For SQA Exams	General Level Exam C Reading

Answer all of the questions.

Read the following passage and then answer the questions. Remember to use your own words as much as possible.

Leckie×Leckie

Scotland's leading educational publishers

Made in America

In this extract from 'Made in America', the writer Bill Bryson describes how McDonald's has grown into a multi-million pound business.

1   As late as 1950, pork was still the most widely eaten meat in America, and by a considerable margin, but over the next two decades the situation was reversed. By 1970 Americans were eating twice as much beef as pork, nearly a hundred pounds of it a year, and half of that in the form of hamburgers. One company more than any other was responsible for this massive change in dietary habits: McDonald's.

2   The story as conveyed by the company is well known. A salesman of Multimixers named Ray Kroc became curious as to why a small hamburger stand on the edge of the desert in San Bernardino, California, would need eight Multimixers – enough to make forty milk-shakes at a time, more than any other restaurant in American could possibly want to make – and decided to fly out and have a look. The restaurant he found, run by the brothers Maurice and Richard McDonald, was small, only 600 square feet, but the burgers were tasty, the fries crisp, the shakes unusually thick, and it was unquestionably popular with the locals. Kroc at this time was fifty-two years old, an age when most men would be thinking of slowing down, but he saw an opportunity here. He bought the McDonald's name and began building an empire. The implication has always been that the original McDonald's was an obscure, rinky-dink operation in the middle of nowhere, and that it was only the towering genius of Ray Kroc that made it into the streamlined, efficient, golden-arched institution that we know and love today. It wasn't entirely like that.

3   By 1954, when Kroc came along, the McDonald brothers were already legendary, at least in the trade. *American Restaurant* magazine had done a cover story on them in 1952, and they were constantly being visited by people who wanted to see how they generated so much turnover from so little space. With sales of over $350,000 a year (all of it going through one busy cash register) and profits above $100,000, McDonald's was one of the most successful restaurants in America. In his autobiography, Kroc makes it sound as if the McDonald brothers had never thought of franchising until he came along. In fact, by the time he visited them they had a dozen franchised operations going.

4   Almost everything later associated with the McDonald's chain was invented or perfected by the brothers, from the method of making French fries to the practice of trumpeting the number of hamburgers sold. As early as 1950, they had a sign outside announcing 'Over 1 Million Sold'. They even came up with the design of a sloping roof, red and white tiled walls and integral golden arches – not for the San Bernardino outlet but for their first franchise operation, which opened in Phoenix in 1952, two years before Kroc came along.

5   The McDonald's were, in short, the true heroes of the fast-food revolution, and by any measure they were remarkable men. They had moved to California from New Hampshire (or possibly Vermont; sources conflict) during the depression years, and opened their first drive-in restaurant in 1937 near Pasadena. It didn't

sell hamburgers. Then in 1940 they opened a new establishment at Fourteenth and E Streets, at the end of Route 66, in San Bernardino in a snug octagonal structure. It was a conventional hamburger stand, and it did reasonably well.

6   In 1948, however, the brothers were seized with a strange vision. They closed the business for three months, fired the twenty carhops, got rid of all the china and silverware, and reopened with a new, entirely novel idea: that the customer would have to come to a window to collect the food rather than have it brought to the car. They cut the menu to just seven items – hamburgers, cheeseburgers, pie, crisps, coffee, milk and pop. Customers no longer specified what they wanted on their hamburgers but received them with ketchup, mustard, onions and pickle. The hamburgers were made smaller – just ten to a pound – but the price was halved to fifteen cents each.

7   The change was a flop. Business fell by 80 per cent. The teenagers on whom they had relied went elsewhere. Gradually, however, a new type of clientele developed, the family, particularly after they added French fries and milk shakes to the menu, and even more particularly when customers realised that the food was great and that you could feed a whole family for a few dollars. Before long McDonald's had almost more business than it could handle.

8   As volume grew, the brothers constantly refined the process to make the production of food more streamlined and efficient. With a local machine-shop owner named Ed Toman they invented almost everything connected with the production of fast food, from dispensers that pump out a precise dollop of ketchup or mustard to the Lazy Susans on which twenty-four hamburger buns can be speedily dressed. They introduced the idea of specialization – one person who did nothing but cook hamburgers, another who make shakes, another to dress the buns, and so on – and developed the now universal practice of having the food prepared and waiting so that customers could place an order and immediately collect it.

franchising   selling a licence to an individual who can then use a company's name and sell its products.

		Marks	

1. (a) What changed in the American diet between 1950 and 1970?

_____

_____ | 2 | 1 | 0 |

(b) Which company was responsible for this change? Quote to support your answer.

_____

_____ | 2 | 1 | 0 |

2. 'as conveyed by the company'. What does this expression tell you about the writer's attitude towards McDonald's?

_____

_____ | 2 | 1 | 0 |

3. Why was Ray Kroc curious about the 'small hamburger stand' in California?

_____

_____ | 2 | ■ | 0 |

4. What made the restaurant popular, according to Ray Kroc?

_____

_____ | 2 | 1 | 0 |

5. Why does the writer mention Ray Kroc's age? Answer in your own words.

_____

_____ | 2 | 1 | 0 |

6. (a) The writer suggests that McDonald's was originally a 'rinky-dink operation'. (paragraph 2) Explain **in your own words** what this means.

_____

_____ | 2 | ■ | 0 |

(b) Give an example of a word later in the paragraph which <u>contrasts</u> with this idea.

[   ] | 2 | ■ | 0 |

7. By 1954, the McDonald brothers were already famous. Give **two** pieces of evidence from the text to support this claim.

(a) _____

(b) _____ | 2 | 1 | 0 |

	Marks	

8. Why do you think Ray Kroc might want people to think that he was the first person to think of buying a McDonald's franchise?

_____

_____ 2 1 0

9. 'trumpeting the number of hamburgers sold' (paragraph 4).

(_a_) What **technique** does the writer use here and what does it tell you about how McDonald's communicated its huge sales numbers?

_____

_____ 2 1 0

(_b_) Give an example of how McDonald's were 'trumpeting' the numbers of hamburgers sold.

_____

_____ 2 1 0

10. Read paragraph 3 again. What happened in both 1952 and 1954?

1952 _____

1954 _____ 2 1 0

11. Write down **two** expressions the writer uses in paragraph 5 to show that he admires the McDonald brothers.

(_a_) _____

(_b_) _____ 2 1 0

12. In 1948, the McDonald brothers had a 'strange vision'. (paragraph 6)

(_a_) What was their 'strange vision'?

_____

_____ 2 1 0

(_b_) Name two changes the brothers made to the menu in 1948.

(i) _____

(ii) _____ 2 1 0

(c) Write down an expression from paragraph 5 which means the same as 'original'.

_____ 2 ■ 0

13. Why are dashes used around the expration '– just ten to the pound –'.(paragraph 6)

_____

_____ 2 1 0

	Marks	

14. 'The change was a flop'. (paragraph 7) Comment on the word choice in this sentence.

_____

_____

2   1   0

15. To whom did the new McDonalds restaurants appeal and why?

_____

_____

2   1   0

16. As the business grew, what did the brothers do to make food production more efficient?

_____

_____

2   1   0

Think about the passage as a whole.

17. (*a*) Do you think customers enjoyed eating at McDonald's? Answer fully, referring to the passage to support your answer.

_____

_____

2   1   0

(*b*) Do you think employees enjoyed working at McDonald's? Answer fully, referring to the passage to support your answer.

_____

_____

2   1   0

18. In your opinion, what is the purpose of this extract? Tick the purpose you think best fits the extract. Give a reason for your answer.

(*a*) To advertise McDonald's   ☐

(*b*) To criticize how McDonald's is run   ☐

(*c*) To give the true story about McDonald's   ☐

_____

_____

2   1   0

19. This extract comes from a chapter entitled 'Welcome to the Space Age: The 1950s and Beyond'. Do you find this title appropriate? Give a reason for your answer

_____

_____

2   1   0

English   Standard Grade: Foundation and General

Practice Papers
For SQA Exams

**Foundation and General Level
Writing**

Read these instructions first.

1. Use the photographs and words to help you think about what to write. Look at it all and consider carefully all possibilities.

2. There are 21 questions to choose from.

3. Decide which **one** you will answer.
   Then write the number is the margin of your answer.

4. Think carefully about the wording of your chosen question.
   Make a **plan** before you start writing.
   Re-read your answer before you finish.
   Mark any changes **neatly**.

Scotland's leading educational publishers

PRACTICE WRITING PAPER

FIRST   Look at the photograph below. It shows a train leaving a station.

NEXT   Think about going on a journey.

1. Write about a journey or trip you have made. Remember to include your thoughts and feelings.

2. Write a short story about a character who makes a train journey. You should develop setting, character and plot.

3. Write a letter of complaint to a train company about poor service.

FIRST   Look at the photograph below. It shows a baby in a pram.

NEXT   Think about family.

4.   Write about your experience of a new baby in the family. Remember to include your thoughts and feelings.

5.   Over 9000 babies are born each year in Scotland to mothers aged between 13 and 19. Give your views.

6.   'Bringing Up Baby.' Write in any way you like using this title.

FIRST   Look at the picture below. It shows a futuristic city.

NEXT   Think about the future.

7. Write a short story using the following opening:
    He emerged from the time machine and looked out over a strange crystal city he did not recognise. The buildings shone brightly but there was no movement. No life.

8. Write about your hopes and dreams for the future.

9. Mobile phones – a nuisance or an essential piece of technology? Give your views.

10. Write in any way you like about the picture above.

FIRST   Look at the photograph below. It shows a school football match.

NEXT   Think about sporting and leisure activities.

11. Write a letter to your local newspaper to complain about the lack of sporting/ leisure facilities in your community.

12. Write a short story about a sporting champion who loses a match/game at a crucial time. You should develop setting, character and plot.

13. The Scottish Government wants to encourage school pupils to be healthy, for example, by providing healthy school dinners and encouraging pupils to take PE. Give your views.

FIRST   Look at the photo below of a busker.

NEXT   Think about different kinds of music.

14. Write a short story about a busker. You should develop setting, character and plot.

15. Write about the music you enjoy and what it means to you.

16. 'Pop is actually my least favourite kind of music because it lacks real depth.' (Christina Aguilera) Give your views.

The following questions do not have any photographs.

17. Zoos are cruel and inhumane. Give your views.

18. 'You've got a friend.' Write in any way you like about friendship.

19. Describe the scene brought to mind by one of the following:
'A full moon hangs, a round, white blaze.'
OR
'Bare branches in winter are a form of writing.'

20. Write a short story in which the main character makes a life-changing decision. You should develop setting and character as well as plot.

21. 'It wasn't us!' Write about an experience you have had when you were part of a group blamed for something.

Worked Answers

Foundation – Mamo and Tiggist

MARKING SCHEME

1. (they live in) a shack
    no lighting
    corrugated-iron roof
    ragged blanket
    (bare) straw mattress

    Any three = 2; any two = 1.

> **HINT**
> Keep it short! The question asks for 'pieces of evidence'; you don't need to explain anything.

> **TOP EXAM TIP**
> Remember to read the information in italics before the actual passage begins It is there to help you. In this case, you are told quite a lot about the characters and their situation.

2. hadn't felt much about it (2)

> **HINT**
> When asked for 'an expression', keep it as short as possible – never more than five or six words.

> **TOP EXAM TIP**
> Remember to read all the paragraphs for the question – in this case there are four question based on six paragraphs. The questions will probably go through the paragraphs in order, but you should read all the paragraphs before attempting any of the questions.

3. close/loving/affectionate/protective/maternal (2)

> **HINT**
> You are being asked about the 'relationship' (the way they behave towards each other) so you need to do more than repeat what they say or do. Although there is space to write quite a lot, you would in fact get the 2 marks for a single word such as 'protective'.

> **TOP EXAM TIP**
> Notice that the marks for this question are 2 or 0. This means there will be a single important idea to look for.

4. his stomach suddenly contracting (2)

> **TOP EXAM TIP**
> 'Expression' – keep it short!

5. she answers 'I don't know' twice (1) which suggests she is negative, unhelpful, uncooperative, off-putting, etc (1)

> **HINT** There are really two parts to this question: what Tiggist's responses are *and* your 'description' of them.

> **TOP EXAM TIP**
> If you're asked about the way a character is feeling, try to put yourself in the character's place.

6. depressed, miserable, worried, despairing, sad, negative, pessimistic

> **HINT** This is very like question 3: a 2 or 0 question which can be answered very briefly.

7. made him feel small, uncomfortable, insecure, … (1)
   made his skin tingle, come out in goosebumps, feel shivery, … (1)

> **HINT** In this question, there are two key expressions: 'shrivelled him up' and 'skin was prickling all over'. To score marks, you need to find some other way of getting these ideas across.

8. any two of the following (quote or description/explanation):

   'What do you think?'
   'Oh, shut up Mamo'
   'How do I know?'
   'Work it out for yourself.'
   the sharpness in her voice

> **HINT** The important word in the question is 'impatient'. Make sure the details you choose are obviously connected to the idea of being impatient.

9. he is too frightened/doesn't want to make Tiggist angrier/ doesn't want to hear the answer/knows it will be upsetting (2)

> **HINT** This is a 'Why' question, which means you'll have to come up with a reason based on what you've read, but like questions 3 and 6, this is for 2 or 0, so you can assume there is one basic point being looked for.

> **TOP EXAM TIP**
> 'Why …?' is one of the most common types of question. The explanation you are looking for will always be in the passage – you will not be expected to have 'outside knowledge'.

10. shock/anger at the idea of her not being with him/looking after him

> **HINT** Very similar to the last question, but here you'll have to 'read between the lines' a little: what is it about what Tiggist says that makes Mamo move away? Put yourself in his position and imagine the effect her words would have.

11. (*a*) because she is saying she'll look after him (1) but her voice shows she is not sure (1)

or

because he could tell she was not definite about going to look after him (2)

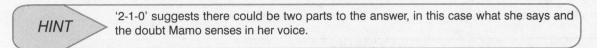

> **HINT** '2-1-0' suggests there could be two parts to the answer, in this case what she says and the doubt Mamo senses in her voice.

(*b*) 1. rolled away
2. took blanket
3. clenched fists

all three = 2; any two = 1

> **HINT** Keep it short! The question asks for 'pieces of evidence', not for any explanation.

12. (*a*) assumed (2)

TOP EXAM TIP

'One word' means exactly that! Do not try to squeeze other words into the box.

(*b*) rustle up (the money) (1)
scrape (together) (1)

> **HINT** Don't write down everything that's said about money – pick out the key words, in this case 'rustle up' and 'scrape'.

13. nervous/uncertain/frightened, etc (2)

> **HINT** Think beyond what 'muttered' *means* (mumbled or spoke unclearly) and ask yourself *why* Mamo does this, how he is feeling.

TOP EXAM TIP

If you see the word 'suggest' in a question about an individual word, you are being asked to go beyond what a word *means*.

14. (*a*) basic idea that she thinks it won't work (1)
additional point that she is being contemptuous/thinks it's unrealistic/ stupid (1)

> **HINT** A bit like the last question: not so much *what* she did as *why*, and what this tells you about her attitude to Mamo's suggestion.

(*b*) lack of money (1)
difficulty in getting a pitch (1)

> **HINT** Notice it's '2-1-0' so there could be two reasons.

15. any two of:

> warmth
> bright morning air
> bright light
> breakfast fires

TOP EXAM TIP

Be careful: questions 15, 16 and 17 are introduced with the instruction 'Look at Paragraphs 28 to 30', but for question 15 you must answer from Paragraph 28 only.

16. no money to pay fees/can't afford it/too poor

TOP EXAM TIP

A very easy question! Don't worry that it seems 'too easy' – no one is trying to trick you or lead you into a trap.

17. he thinks they might be a source of help to him/unlike the children, he can get something from them (2)

HINT

The quotation in the question is from the start of the paragraph, but remember to read the whole paragraph – especially since in this case the answer is clearly spelled out in the last few words.

18. 'Yes' could be supported by any two of:
> clean face and hands (1)
> tidy hair (1)
> evidence of attempt to clean skirt (1)

> 'No' could be supported by:
> stains on skirt (1)
> nervousness/stiffness (1)

HINT

For practice, try to answer this question both ways: even if you thought the answer was 'Yes', can you think of answers for 'No'? Try this for similar questions, eg question 21 in this practice paper.

TOP EXAM TIP

In questions like this, you won't get marks for your choice of 'Yes' or 'No' – it's your explanation that matters.

19. (i) the company of other boys (1)

(ii) his love of music (1)

TOP EXAM TIP

'main' in the questions means there might be more than one reason, but you are being asked to decide which is the most important.

20. (*a*) metaphor (2)

> **HINT** He is not literally 'drinking', since melodies (tunes) can't be drunk, so this must be a metaphor (it's not a simile, since it doesn't use 'like' or 'as').

> ### TOP EXAM TIP
>
> Before the exam, make sure you know the most important technical terms: simile, metaphor, personification, alliteration, onomatopoeia, rhyme, …

(*b*) simple point that he liked it, etc (1)

more sophisticated point, eg that he soaked it up, it was important to him, it sustained/refreshed him/was as precious as water, etc (2)

> **HINT** This type of question is difficult; the best way to approach it is to think what the word *really* means (the 'literal' meaning) and then try to see how this is connected with what the writer is describing. Here, 'drinking' suggests something refreshing, something important to keeping you alive, etc, so to Mamo music is really important and pleasant.

21. could be either answer; any two relevant quotes/pieces of textual evidence relevant to the choice made (1) + (1)

> **HINT** As with question 18, it's not your choice that matters, it's your explanation.
>
> Ideas to support 'better': Tiggist might get a job; the optimistic mood in the morning; Tiggist has always looked out for Mamo; without drunken mother, things might be easier;
>
> Ideas to support 'worse': they might be thrown out their home; they might be split up; Tiggist might fail to get the job; without education, Mamo will find things difficult;

> ### TOP EXAM TIP
>
> Try looking at the last question before you start on any of the questions! The last question often asks you to 'think about the passage as a whole', so if you know at the beginning what it is you'll have to know about the whole passage, you might be able to think about it while you are answering the other questions. This way you'll maybe have some good ideas for the last question without having to read the whole passage again.

1.   conserve (2)

>
> *HINT* Although in this case the answer comes quite early in the paragraph, you should always read the whole paragraph before you decide which word to choose.

TOP EXAM TIP

'One word' means exactly that! Do not try to squeeze other words into the box.

2.   magical (1)   beautiful (1)

> *HINT* The key words in the question are 'positive impression'. You're not being asked just for words which describe the owls, so 'rare' will not do, since that doesn't convey are 'positive impression'. (The word 'touched' *could* possibly be said to create a positive impression of the owls since it shows the effect they have on people who see them, but it is much wiser to go for the obvious choices.)

3.   host (2)

> *HINT* You might be more familiar with 'host' as meaning the person in charge (the host of a party, the host of a game show), but it also means 'a large number' (or an army). Sensible reading of the paragraph shows there's really only one possible answer.

TOP EXAM TIP

When you're looking for a single word you might sometimes have to rely on a common sense 'guess'. (As Sherlock Holmes said: 'When you've eliminated the impossible, whatever remains, however improbable, must be the truth.')

4.   unreliable (2)

TOP EXAM TIP

If you're asked to 'find a word that means the same as ...' and you can't spot it right away, take the possible answers and see how each of them sounds in place of the given word. This will often make the correct answer obvious.

5.   Any two of:
   • quite likely   • might have
   • (we shall) never know   • may have only

TOP EXAM TIP

When asked for 'an expression', keep it as short as possible – never more than five or six words.

6. Explanation of idea(s) contained in 'mechanisation of farming' and/or 'intensive', eg more machinery was used (1) in the production of food/cultivation of the land (1) which was done in a more focused/rigorous/demanding way (1). [Straight lift: 0]

HINT

After five straightforward questions all of which asked you to quote, all of a sudden you are asked to **explain** something in **your own words**. It is important that you make the shift from quoting to explaining.

For this question, the key words in the passage are 'mechanisation' and 'intensive' and you have to find some way of expressing these ideas in different words. (You have to make it clear to the examiner that you know what these words mean – if you simply quote, then the examiner won't know (and won't give you any marks!).

TOP EXAM TIP

If the question says 'in your own words' you must not simply quote from the passage. It usually means there is a key word or expression for you to find, but in order to show you understand what it means you have to put it into different words.

7. (a) To get rid of mice and rats/pests/vermin (2)
   (b) It provided shelter (1) and warmth (1)

HINT

There is no stated requirement here to use your own words, but it's always better to try – in fact, here it would be very difficult to answer the question just by quoting. You don't have to find another word for 'mice' or for 'rats', but summarising them as 'pests' or 'vermin' shows really good understanding.

TOP EXAM TIP

If it doesn't say 'in your own words', it is still much wiser to do so. Only if you're specifically told to quote can you do so safely. Certainly, you should never be copying large chunks from the passage.

8. (a) Explanation of idea contained in 'drive to be more self-sufficient', e.g. the need to produce as much food as possible (1) in this country/ without having to import (1)

HINT

Notice it's a 2-1-0 question, which suggests there are two ideas being looked for, in this case the need to produce a lot of food and to do so without importing.

TOP EXAM TIP

Remember: 'own words' means find the key words and 'translate' them.

   (b) Explanation in own words of any one of the following (2) [Straight lift: 0]:
   'human population expansion'
   'government policies'
   'consumer pressure for ever cheaper food'

HINT

There are actually three reasons – choose the one you find easiest to put into your own words.

9. (*a*) It introduces/gives an expansion/more detail (1) about the 'other factors' (1)

(*b*) It divides up/separates the items (1) in the list (of other factors) (1)

> **HINT** Remember to describe what the punctuation is doing in *this* paragraph in *this* passage; don't just give a general definition of what the punctuation usually does.

TOP EXAM TIP

Before the exam, revise the key punctuation marks: comma, colon, semicolon, brackets, dashes, dash, exclamation mark.

Always be specific when describing what punctuation is doing.

10. (*a*) True (2)

The first sentence clearly identifies three measures.

(*b*) False (2)

False because it says 'most of these can be prevented', i.e. not all.

(*c*) Can't Tell (2)

Tricky, but the correct answer is 'Can't Tell' because although we're told that 'Steps can ... be taken to maximise nesting success' and that 'this has been a major part of the Barn Owl Trust's work since 1997', there's no indication about how successful they have been.

TOP EXAM TIP

Don't agonise too long about 'True/False/Can't Tell' questions. If you think about them too long, you can end up doubting your own judgement!

11. giving advice about owls (2)

> **HINT** The words 'main topic' in the question suggest there are several topics – you have to decide which is the most important. The three 'wrong' answers (called 'distractors' in a multiple-choice question) are not ridiculous – they are all referred to in the paragraph – but the 'main' topic has to be about giving advice.

TOP EXAM TIP

For this type of question make sure you read the whole paragraph before making your choice. (Try covering up all the options and deciding for yourself what the main topic is.)

12. (*a*) Basic explanation (1) or clear explanation (2) of any one of the following [Straight lift: 0]:

- 'erect safer nestboxes...'
- 'make alternative provision...'
- '...special floats...'

TOP EXAM TIP

As with question 8(b), you have three choices – choose the one you find easiest to explain in your own words.

(*b*) Telling/suggesting opposed to actually doing (2)

> **HINT** Use you understanding of 'practical' from the last question to help you see the difference – one is actually doing things 'hands-on'; the other is telling others what to do.

13. Any two of:
- impressive (track record)
- highly committed
- excellent (reputation)
- very active (volunteers)

 HINT Identify more than two possibilities and then choose the two best.

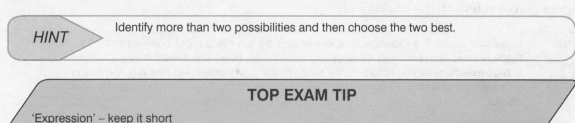

TOP EXAM TIP

'Expression' – keep it short

14. Making a joke/play on words (1) about birth of organisation using term associated with birds (1)

HINT Try thinking about the way it would be read out loud. This way you might get some sense of the little joke involved. (Exams might not be the best time to be thinking of humour, but some of the Close Reading passages do contain a little light humour.)

TOP EXAM TIP

As with questions 9(a) and (b), don't just give your standard 'this-is-what-inverted-commas-always-do' answer. In fact, that would not be much use here. Always be alert to what is going on at *this* point in *this* passage.

15. It has brought about positive (1) changes in Local Authority policies (1) [Accept lift]

HINT 'evidence' suggests a specific bit of information; the question is not clear about whether or not to use 'own words' so you should try not to quote (or 'lift') too much. In fact, in this question a lift is acceptable – largely because it would be very difficult to 'translate' the key idea.

16. (A team of) professional staff

 HINT You probably recognise that 'professional' in this context means 'paid' (as in professional footballer or professional musician), so the contrast with 'voluntary' should be obvious.

17. (*a*) Shows the extent/range/large number (1) of the Trust's activities (1)
(*b*) Creates climax (1) to emphasise the importance of the Trust (1)

 HINT You've been told what the features are (often you have to identify them for yourself), so all your effort has to go into describing the effect. Avoid vague answers about what *any* list does – what does *this* list do? Not what *any* delayed subject does, but what does *this* delayed subject do? Notice that in both answers you must refer to the work of the Barn Owl Trust.

TOP EXAM TIP

When answering on Sentence Structure, never lose sight of **meaning** – what's going on in *this* sentence in *this* passage.

18. (i) Accept either; no marks for choice

    (ii) One appropriate specific reference in support of choice (1)

        Two appropriate specific references in support of choice **or** an appropriate general overview of the passage (2)

HINT

Questions about 'the Passage as a whole' can be a bit scary, but don't be put off by them. No one is asking you do anything impossible. Read the question very carefully and do exactly what you're told to do. Your opinion is important. No one is going to say your opinion is wrong – you will be marked according to how well you support your opinion.

TOP EXAM TIP

Try looking at the last question before you start on any of the questions! The last question often asks you to 'think about the passage as a whole', so if you know at the beginning what it is you'll have to know about the whole passage, you might be able to think about it while you are answering the other questions. This way you will maybe have some good ideas for the last question without having to read the whole passage again.

PRACTICE EXAM B　　　　**FOUNDATION LEVEL WORKED ANSWERS**

1. Marmie/Floella's mother (1)

    ten days (1)

TOP EXAM TIP

The first question is usually near the beginning of the passage. Did you find where it says 'after just ten days of being in England'?

---

2. They rushed to her (1)

    OR

    They touched her (1)

    OR

    They ran away from her (1)

    OR

    They laughed at her (1)

HINT

Paragraph 2 starts with the words 'When I arrived at school, many of the children....' <u>After</u> this phrase, you will find the answer!

TOP EXAM TIP

In this question, there are two marks available. Usually, two marks means you should write two ideas/pieces of information. You get one mark for each idea here. How many did you get?

3. She thought they were being nice to her (1) but they were laughing at her/being nasty to her/making a fool of her /she was different (1)

TOP EXAM TIP

The first three questions here are 'understanding' questions – they ask you about ideas or information in the passage.

In any question, it is useful to highlight the key word or phrase in it – some pupils like to use a highlighter for this. Here you might have highlighted 'Floella think' and 'paying attention' and 'real reason'. This can help you to focus on what you are looking for in the passage.

4. No (1) – it was a 'novelty' (1)

HINT Did you find the sentence in the passage which tells you the answer to question 4 starting 'At that time…'? Something new is a 'novelty'; in other words, the children had not seen someone like Floella before.

TOP EXAM TIP

The phrase 'Quote from the passage to support your answer' always means that you have to write down a word (or words) from the passage which show the examiner where you 'found' your answer.

5.
The school was partly enclosed by high wire fencing	false
Children had marked out a hopscotch game	cannot tell
A bull's eye pattern was painted on one of the walls	true
There were letters engraved above the main door	true

HINT In the lines from 'It was surrounded…' to '… what they meant', you will find all the information you need to tick the boxes.

The school was 'surrounded' by fencing which means the fence was built all the way round the school - so number 1 is 'false'.

The passage does not tell you who marked out the hopscotch game so number 2 is 'cannot tell'.

Numbers 3 and 4 are true – did you find them easily?

6. The walls were tiled halfway up (1) OR the building felt cold OR 'making the building feel cold' (1) OR 'mushy green' paint had been used (1) OR paint was 'flaking off' (1) OR paint had been 'scratched' (1) OR 'ceilings were 'dull beige' (1) OR floorboards were 'worn' (1) OR floorboards were 'splintering' (1)

HINT Did you notice there are two marks here? You are asked to write down three pieces of evidence. It works like this.

Three pieces of evidence = two marks

Two pieces of evidence = one mark

One piece of evidence = no marks

7. Difference = classrooms had partitions, not walls (1)
Similarity = desks and blackboards were the same (1)

8. Floella knew about it/had seen it (1) and it was typical/common/happened very day/it was regular/a pattern (1)

> **TOP EXAM TIP**
>
> You will gain one mark for explaining what 'familiar' means and one mark for explaining what 'routine' means. If you did not know either of these words, could you work this out from the sentence starting 'The structure of the day..'? In this sentence, the school day is described; '... lessons, playtime, more lessons. lunch and play, then ending the day with more lessons.' This might help you to work out the meaning of 'familiar routine' as it shows that what happened during the school day was always the same.

9. She could not understand her accent/what she said (1) and this was surprising because Floella found the work easy/was not stupid/was not an idiot (1)

> **HINT**
>
> The first part of the answer is easy to find because it comes after the phrase 'Yet the teacher treated me like an idiot because…'.
>
> The answer to why this was surprising is written in the sentence before this one – 'The work the teacher game us was so easy and simple...'
>
> So always look BEFORE and AFTER the key phrase or word to find an answer.

10. Simile (1)

It tells us that she felt out of place/she did not fit in/she did not feel secure/she was in a strange environment (1)

> **TOP EXAM TIP**
>
> There is usually a question about imagery at Foundation level – this could be metaphor or simile or personification. Learn about images and why they are used so you are able to answer these image questions!
>
> In this question, did you know 'like a fish out of water' is a simile because it uses the word 'like' and because Floella is <u>comparing</u> herself to a fish?

11. (*a*) Milk was cold (1)

OR

Milk was in small glass bottle (1)

OR

Used straw (1)

OR

Had silver foil top (1)

OR

Creamy liquid (1)

> **HINT**
>
> Did you use the highlighting technique in question 11 to focus on the phrase 'new and exciting'? The answers come AFTER this phrase in the passage.

(*b*) She did not like the thick/furry feeling/taste in her mouth (2)

12. She felt part of the game/included/secure/comfortable (2)

TOP EXAM TIP

If you are asked to answer in your own words, you will not get any marks for quoting. So if you wrote 'at home' for your answer, you would be given no marks! You have to explain the phrase 'at home' using other words.

This is a difficult question, so you get two marks if you get it right!

13. (a) Boys spat at her (1) OR called her names (1) OR made aggressive faces at her (1) OR told her she was not welcome (1) OR laughed at her (1)

   (b) It is not appropriate because 'game' usually means a happy/fun/enjoyable activity (1) and this game was wrong/cruel/unpleasant/not happy/hurtful (1)

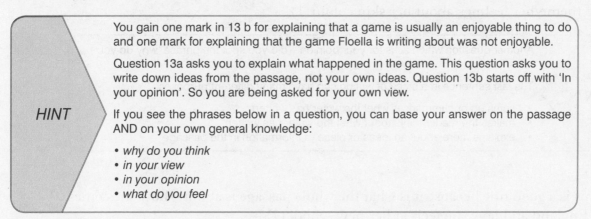

HINT

You gain one mark in 13 b for explaining that a game is usually an enjoyable thing to do and one mark for explaining that the game Floella is writing about was not enjoyable.

Question 13a asks you to explain what happened in the game. This question asks you to write down ideas from the passage, not your own ideas. Question 13b starts off with 'In your opinion'. So you are being asked for your own view.

If you see the phrases below in a question, you can base your answer on the passage AND on your own general knowledge:

• why do you think
• in your view
• in your opinion
• what do you feel

14. These are the words the boys used/she is quoting what the boys said (2)

TOP EXAM TIP

You are not asked to explain what 'my kind' means and so explaining what it means will gain no marks. You are being asked about why the writer has used inverted commas (sometimes called quotations marks). Do you know why they are used?

Writers use inverted commas (sometimes called quotation marks)

• to show that the word(s) has been spoken or used by someone else
• to show that the writer is being sarcastic (by using the word but meaning the opposite!)
• to show speech e.g. in fiction writing

Do you know why writers use these?

• commas
• inverted commas
• brackets
• dashes

There might be a question about any of these so find out why and when they are used!

15. (a) 'confused and baffled' OR 'like a trapped helpless creature' (2)

   (b) 'angry and violent' (2)

TOP EXAM TIP

You are asked to quote a phrase and not a word. So you would not get a mark for quoting 'confused' on its own or for quoting 'baffled' on its own. A phrase is two words or more!

16. Her mother was away/not at home/not able to care for the children/not there for her children/her mother was not available (1)
AND
She had to grow up/manage without her mother/look after the younger children/ be more mature/do things for herself/do things without her mother's help (1)

17. To be strong (1)
OR
To make something of themselves (1)
OR
Not to let them get the better of the children (1)

18. It sums up/summarises/says in one sentence (1) what the passage has been about/ the theme/her feelings about her skin colour(1)

> **HINT**
>
> Another question which asks for your opinion – did you spot the phrase 'why do you think'?
>
> The last sentence in a piece of writing can have many different purposes:
>
> • sums up or summarises what the writer has written
> • makes the reader think about what the writer has written
> • explains more about an ideas or piece of information in the passage

19. This is a good title because it is what the whole passage is about – how she comes to England and how she feels at her new school (2)
OR
This is not a good title as the passage only tells us about her school and I think 'settling in' means getting used to lots of things, not just school. (2)

> **TOP EXAM TIP**
>
> There are two example answers here because there is no right or wrong answer! You could say that it is a good title or you might not think it is a good title. This is up to you! Remember, though, that you have to give a reason for your answer to have a chance of full marks.

PRACTICE EXAM B   GENERAL LEVEL WORKED ANSWERS

1. He remembered being an outsider (2)
OR
He remembered nothing except being an outsider (2)

> **HINT**   Usually, the first question is not too difficult. This question asks you to explain the second sentence in the paragraph; 'Daniel had no memories other than of being an outsider'.

2. It was his birthday (1) and it was his first day at school (1)

HINT — Some pupils find it helpful to underline key words in the questions to help them to focus on what is being looked for. In this question, the key phrase is the date '3rd of March 1767' and the key word is 'important'. So you know that you are looking for information about that date – which is found easily in paragraph 2.

TOP EXAM TIP

Questions will usually follow the order of the passage. So, the first questions will usually ask you about the first few sentences or paragraphs of the passage. Then the questions will work through the passage chronologically (in the order in which the events happened). Examiners write questions in this way to make things easier for you – so you will not have to 'jump around' the passage to find the answers you are looking for!

3. He did not answer when asked to read a simple word (2)
    OR
    The teacher thought he could not read (2)
    OR
    He did not know/understand what the teacher wanted him to do (2)

HINT — Again, it may be helpful to underline key words in the questions to help you to focus on what is being looked for. In this question, the key phrase is 'the teachers... thought' and the key word is 'stupid'. So you know that you are looking for information about the teachers at the school and for an example of something Daniel did which the teachers might have thought was stupid.

TOP EXAM TIP

This is what we call an 'understanding' question – these ask you to explain ideas in the passage. Question 1 was also an 'understanding' question.

In question 2, you are asked to explain in your own words so there is no need to quote. And sometimes you are asked to quote so there is no need to use your own words! If you are ever not sure whether to quote or use your own words, do both.

4. She spanked/beat/hit him (2)

HINT — The key word in the question is 'reacted' – in other words, how did Mrs Bartholemew behave when Daniel did not answer. Find the sentence in the passage where the teacher shows him the engraving. The answer is actually four sentences later.

5. Daniel was more interested in... concentrating on his own special numbers (2)
    OR
    Multiplication tables were too easy for Daniel (2)

HINT — In the passage, find the sentence which tells you that Daniel was not interested in multiplication. Did you spot it? The answer is in the next sentence.

TOP EXAM TIP

You will often be asked about an idea in the passage but you have to answer 'in your own words'. Many pupils answer these questions by quoting the exact words from the passage. You will not be given any marks for doing this. For example, if you had written for this answer 'he was collecting his special numbers' or 'he was looking under the desk' you would be given no marks as you have simply copied these phrases from the passage.

6.   He was lonely/alone/on his own/friendless/a loner (2)

HINT

This question is easy if you know the meaning of the word 'solitary' which means alone. If you did not know this, could you have made a guess based on what you have learned about Daniel from the passage? It's also always worth checking the glossary in case a definition is given there, as it is in this case. If you are not sure of an answer, think about it but don't spend too long on it. If you are really stuck, leave it and come back to it when you have finished the rest of the questions. Sometimes, just working through other questions and answers will help you in understanding the passage – and can mean you finally 'get' that difficult question!

TOP EXAM TIP

Did you notice that you did not have to make two points in your answer this time – even though the question is worth two marks? Sometimes, examiners give two marks for an answer to a difficult question. This can make it tricky sometimes to work out how much to write, but working through this book will help you. If you do not give the correct answer you will be given 0 marks.

7.   She 'pounced' (1) on him meaning that she swooped down/jumped on him suddenly (1)
    OR
    She suddenly grabbed/pulled with force/grasped (1) the notebook; this is shown by the word 'seized' (1)

HINT

You are being asked here to explain and quote from the passage. Look at the two suggested answers again – the first answer quotes first then explains. The second answer explains then quotes. Try answering in both ways and find out which order you prefer.

8.   She was interested/intrigued/concerned/angry/wanted to know more about what was in the notebook/his ability in Maths (1)
    AND
    She took it to look at later/show to someone else/so he could not look at it in class (1)

HINT

This question asks for your opinion – the key phrase in the question is 'Why do you think...'.

Of course, your answer must be based on your understanding of the passage – as well as your general knowledge. In this case, you can probably work out that the teacher felt an emotion when she looked at the book – concern, anger, curiosity? She wanted to know more about what was in the notebook (remember that earlier in the passage, you read that it had special numbers in it) and you can guess that she might want to show it to someone else/another teacher/look at it again later for herself.

9. He wanted it back because it was special to him/belonged to him (1); we are told it was 'precious' (1)

OR

He did not need it back because the numbers were 'in his head' (1)– he knew them off by heart/for himself (1)

HINT You are being asked here to answer in your own words <u>and</u> support your opinion by using evidence from the passage. Look at the two suggested answers again – the first answer quotes from the passage first then explains. The second answer explains then quotes. Try answering in both ways and find out which order you prefer.

TOP EXAM TIP

Examiners use different ways of asking you to quote from the passage in an answer.

Look at the phrases below and get to know them – they are all asking you to refer back to the passage and quote!

- *Quote from the passage...*
- *Which word/phrase...?*
- *Give an example...*
- *Refer closely to the passage...*

- *Identify the word(s)...*
- *Write down the word(s)...*
- *What expression...?*

10. Daniel was clean and smart (1)

OR

His sisters had been taken out of the house/sent away (1)

OR

His parents were waiting anxiously (1)

OR

They were waiting in the parlour (1)

OR

Daniel's parents did not show any emotion (1)

TOP EXAM TIP

Always 'have a go' at a question. You may feel you have no idea what the answer is but if you write nothing, you will gain no marks! If you write an answer, you just might be correct so never leave an answer blank.

11. He ran to his room and fetched a grid with numbers (1)

AND/OR

He discussed the numbers with Dr Adair excitedly (1)

AND/OR

He shared his book with Dr Adair (1)

AND/OR

He asked Dr Adair for something (1)

HINT To answer this question correctly, you need to work out the meaning of 'in awe'. If you know this phrase means 'in admiration' or 'showing great respect', well done! When you do not know the meaning of a word or phrase, try to work out the meaning by looking at the other words and phrases AROUND it. You are then looking for something that Daniel does which shows us that he behaved normally and NOT formally or by being overpolite. You get one mark for each point you make up to a maximum of two.

12. This is a long sentence with several phrases/divided by commas (1) which reflects/ copies/sounds like how Daniel was speaking. (1)

HINT

This is an 'analysis' question that asks you to think about the writer's craft. In other words, you are being asked about HOW the writer has placed the words in this sentence (and why).

Any question which asks you about word choice or sentence structure is an 'analysis' question.

When answering analysis questions, many pupils only explain WHAT the sentence means. You should explain what it means <u>and</u> write about the structure or word choice to have a chance of full marks.

In this question you are asked about what is unusual in the sentence structure. Here it is used to look and sound like the boy's actual speech.

TOP EXAM TIP

In sentence structure questions, you should comment on:

how the writer has chosen to punctuate the sentence

and/or

how long or short the sentence is and why

and/or

the pattern of the sentence and why it has been written in this way

13. His father was embarrassed by Daniel. (2)

HINT

You are being asked here to work out the meaning of the phrase 'exposing his oddness to a stranger'. The word 'oddness' means strangeness – if the father thinks his son is behaving strangely in front of a stranger then his feeling is most likely to be embarrassment.

14. His friend will be interested because the grid has been done by such a young child. (2)

OR

His friend will be interested because it 'was created by a boy of seven'. (2)

HINT

This question asks for your opinion – the key phrase in the question is 'Why do you think…'.

Your answer must be based on your understanding of the passage – as well as your general knowledge. In this case, you can probably work out that Dr Adair is surprised or impressed by Daniel's ability in Maths at such a young age.

TOP EXAM TIP

Did you notice that you can gain either two mark or zero marks for your answer here? As in Question 6, you will be given two marks for making only one point.

15. She uses 'he' instead of 'you' (1)

AND/OR

She uses informal, slangy language – 'don't he' (1).

AND/OR

Dr Adair uses formal, polite language (1).

AND/OR

Dr Adair uses a long sentence/she uses a short sentence (1).

AND/OR

Dr Adair uses complex words such as 'acquaintance' (1).

HINT

This is another analysis question – you are being asked about HOW the woman speaks to Daniel – not WHAT she says to him. Did you notice that the answer contains quotes from what she says?

It is important to be able to tell the difference between formal and informal language. Informal (sometimes called 'colloquial' or 'conversational') language is everyday, slangy language, for example, the kind of words you use in the playground or with your friends. Formal language is used for writing and when you are in a formal situation e.g. a job interview, writing a school essay etc.

Formal	Informal
No slang	Slang
Fewer or no abbreviations	Abbreviations (e.g.isn't instead of 'is not')
Complex sentences	Simple sentences
Complex words	Simple words

You gain one mark for each difference, up to a maximum of two.

16. It meant little/nothing to him/it was meaningless (1)

AND/OR

He thought it would be quite like/the same as dame school (1)

AND/OR

He was happy to go to the Academy (1) (no marks for 'blithely')

AND/OR

He was not concerned or worried about the Academy (1)

17. A boy or boys at the school (1)

Because he or they thought Daniel's father's job was unimportant or inferior or embarrassing (1)

TOP EXAM TIP

Looking at the ideas before and after the quote you have been given will help you to find the answer – 'other boys' are mentioned at the beginning of the paragraph and the phrase 'A boy took everything…' follows the quotation.

18. Other pupils laughed at his father's job/position (1).

AND/OR

A boy threw all Daniel's clothes out of the window into the mud (1).

AND/OR

A teacher pulled his ear/caned him for saying he had not thrown the clothes out (1).

AND/OR

A big boy lifted him onto a wall and pushed/prodded him until he had to jump off.

19. (a) He felt comfortable/secure there/it 'fitted' him/it was unusual like him (2)

(b) He felt empty/emotionless/miserable (2)

20. 'a journey between one world and another' (2)

> ### TOP EXAM TIP
>
> The key word 'between' helps you here – between 'one world' (Daniel's home) and 'another' world (Daniel's school).

21. They were proud and pleased that he was attending the Academy (2)

> To answer this question, you have to find the key phrase in the passage which means explaining his true feelings – 'he could not tell them how he felt'. The answer is found BEFORE this phrase at the beginning of the sentence – 'His mother and father were so proud....'

22. (*a*) Metaphor or imagery (2)

> Another analysis question which asks you about the writer's word choice. Did you spot that 'anchored' is a metaphor? Sometimes you will be told that you are analysing a metaphor or simile but – more likely – you will be asked to identify the technique just as you are in this question. Of course, you have to spot that this is an image or specifically, a metaphor!

(*b*) 'Anchored' tells us that he feels secure/supported/safe at home (2).

> ### TOP EXAM TIP
>
> Writers use a number of techniques and you could be asked about any of them. Make sure you can recognise:
>
> - imagery (metaphors or similes or personification)
> - onomatopoeia
> - alliteration

23. This is an effective opening because the writer tells us a lot of detail about the character of Daniel. For example, the writer describes Daniel's ability in Maths; ('his special numbers') and Daniel's personality ('being out of step with the world'). (2)

OR

This is an effective opening because it describes how Daniel is an 'outsider'. For example, how his ability in Maths sets him apart from others and how he is bullied at the Naval Academy because of his 'oddness'. (2)

> **HINT**
>
> To gain the full two marks here, you should give a full and clear explanation making at least two points as well as stating whether you think the opening is effective or not.
>
> The answers given here are examples of how you might answer this question. As always with 'evaluation' questions, base your answer on the passage but include your own opinions. Of course, you could say that you do not think the opening is effective – as long as you can justify your answer with evidence from the passage.
>
> Whatever reasons you give, make sure you use quotes to back up your answer.

1. 'I told him not to' (1)
    AND
    'I knew it was a bad idea' (1)

> **HINT**   The answer to the first question is usually near the beginning of the passage. Did you notice that the first sentence in the passage is a question – 'Why did my father have to stop?' You can guess that the answer to this question is going to follow after this!

> **TOP EXAM TIP**
>
> In any question, it is useful to highlight the key word or phrase in it – some pupils like to use a highlighter for this. This can help you to focus on what you are looking for in the passage.

2. Southwold (on the Sussex coast) (1)
    AND
    It was the narrrator's birthday (1)

> **HINT**   The information about why the family had been out is at the beginning of paragraph 2 – 'My fifteenth birthday…' Even if you did not recognize this as the name of a town, the phrase 'a small town on the Sussex coast' helps you.

3. 1 walked on the beach
    AND
    2 looked in the shops
    AND
    3 played/lost money in the arcade

> **HINT**   Again, look for phrases which help you – did you spot the phrase '…had spent the afternoon…'? The things the family did come straight after this phrase. Because this is quite an easy question, you only get two marks for getting all three correct!

4. Yes -
    'great' (1)
    AND
    'really happy' (1)

> **HINT**   If you are asked to quote from the passage, remember it is important to quote correctly – spell and write the words exactly as they are used in the passage. And don't forget quotation marks to show these are not your own words.

5. crummy

6.   They would think it was boring (1)
OR
It was not a good place to go (1)
OR
There would be nothing to do (1)
OR
It would not be special (1)

7.   It had multi-coloured/old beach huts (1)
OR
It had old cannons on the cliff(1)
OR
It had a lighthouse/brewery/village green (1)
OR
It looks like something out of a story (1)

 HINT   Always pay close attention to the words you are asked to look at. You will lose marks if you answer from the wrong part of the passage!

8.   The toy is circular (1)
OR
The toy contains animals (1)
OR
The toy contains models of acrobats, clowns etc (1)
AND
The models or the toy moves on its own(1)
OR
The toy is very realistic (1)

HINT   There are two marks here – one for explaining 'circus' and one for explaining the phrase 'comes to life'.

9.   He has already OR earlier OR before this sentence (1)
given lots of reasons OR explained in detail why he likes Southwold (1)

10. strange (1)
heavy (1)
sad (1)
happy (1)
tired (1)
glad (1)

The writer has all these feelings – but you have to tick CONTRASTING feelings. 'Contrasting' means 'opposite' so you would get no marks if you ticked happy and glad which mean the same thing. The contrasting words are sad/happy or sad/glad.

11. There's nothing strange about that

12. The colours of the sunset were very bright (1)
AND
The sky was completely covered with colour (1)

HINT Did you answer correctly? It often helps to 'make a picture' in your mind of what the writer is describing. The writer describes the colours of the sky – could you 'see' the sunset in your mind? Perhaps this helped you to work out what the question meant.

13. You should have ticked 'metaphor' as the raindrops are being compared to needles. The raindrops are the same shape as needles.
Metaphor (1)
The raindrops are narrow OR long OR sharp OR thin (1)

TOP EXAM TIP

You should be able to recognize and explain all four techniques in the list. Ask your teacher if there are any you are not sure of.

14. His hands gripped OR grasped OR held on (1)
tightly OR firmly (1).

TOP EXAM TIP

You will probably be asked to explain the meaning of a word or phrase. If you know the meaning, well done – just explain the meaning in your own words. If you do not know the meaning, look at the words BEFORE and AFTER the word or phrase (this is called the 'context'). These words could help you work out the meaning. Did you notice the phrase 'pulling it around him'? This phrase helps you to work out that he must be holding the jacket so you could guess that 'clenched' is something to do with 'holding'.

15. The father (1)
because he always tries to 'be nice to people'. (1)

HINT The phrase 'Quote from the passage to support your answer' always means that you have to write down a word (or words) from the passage which show the examiner where you 'found' your answer. Here, if you think the father is more likely to pick up the hitchhiker, you are looking for a phrase in the passage which is your reason for choosing the father as the most likely person. Obviously, someone who is 'nice to people' might pick up a hitchhiker on a rainy night!

16. He went to work without brushing his hair (1)
He wore socks that did not match (1)

17. His older brother Eddy died (1)
AND
To explain more about his family (1)
OR
To make you feel sympathy/sorry for the family (1)
OR
This idea may be important later in the story (1)

18. She did not want to have the hitchhiker in the car/she was uneasy about picking up the hitchhiker (1)
AND
The hitchhiker wanted a lift for 20 miles (1)

19. There are three dots (1)
OR
It is a one word sentence with no verb (1)
AND
This means she does not finish what she is saying (1)
OR
This means she pauses (1)
OR
This means she 'trails off' from what she is saying (1)

HINT There are two marks here – one for making a point about the structure and one for saying why it has been used.

TOP EXAM TIP

Did you know why these dots ....are used? They are to show:

- a pause when a character is speaking
- an unfinished thought
- a 'trailing off' into silence

20. It was empty (1)

OR

It was dark (1)

OR

It had no street lights

OR

There were no buildings (1)

OR

It was not safe (1)

HINT This is another 'why do you think' question so you are being asked for your opinion. There are many reasons in this paragraph which tell you that the A12 was not safe - you have to find two of these reasons. There are also reasons given in the following paragraph – for example, that the A12 is only ten miles away from Fairfields. But remember that you are told only to look in paragraph -.

21. practically

22. It is ugly (1)

OR

It has a wall round it (1)

OR

The wall round it has spikes (1)

OR

The wall round it is very high (1)

OR

It has metal gates (1)

HINT You are being asked here about words and phrases which are unpleasant or negative. You are told Fairfields is 'big' but big does not mean unpleasant! Other ideas are unpleasant, for example, a wall with spikes is not very welcoming!

23. To make it sound better (2)

OR

To make it shorter (2)

OR

So the name does not include unpleasant words like 'criminals' or 'insanity' or 'prison' or 'maximum security' (2)

OR

To make it sound more like a hotel (2)

TOP EXAM TIP

You are being asked for your opinion – the text does not tell us why the name has been changed. So you have to think about this yourself and come up with a sensible reason.

---

24. I would not like to visit Southwold – it sounds very old-fashioned. For example, there are beach huts. It also has a prison quite near it called 'East Suffolk Security Prison for the Criminally Insane' and I might not feel safe there.

 HINT This answer is an example of what you could write because there is no right or wrong answer! You could say that you would like to visit or that you would not like to visit. This is up to you! Remember, though, that you have to give reasons for your answer from the passage.

25. The hitchhiker 'didn't turn round' / He had 'long hair over his eyes' so the family could not see his face. I would not pick him up because he does not seem to want to be seen properly. (2)

OR

He 'seemed quite large'/He was 'towering' over the car. These phrases tell me that he was a big man and I might be frightened of him because he was so big.

OR

The car stopped about ten miles from a prison for the 'criminally insane'. I would not pick him up because he might have escaped from the prison and he might be dangerous.

 HINT The last question is almost always a question which asks for your opinion. Here you are asked if you would have picked him up. Anthony Horowitz has told you that the man did not show his face and does not give any details about his appearance and this makes him seem quite frightening. As always with opinion questions, there is no right or wrong answer – as long as you give good reasons for what you decide.

1. (a) In 1950, pork was the most widely eaten/popular meat (1) but, by 1970, Americans were eating twice as much beef as pork (1).

> **HINT**
>
> Questions will usually follow the order of the passage. So the first questions will usually ask you about the first few sentences or paragraphs of the passage. Then the questions will work through the passage. Examiners write questions in this way to make things easier for you – so you will not have to 'jump around' to find the answers you are looking for!

TOP EXAM TIP

Usually, the first question is not too difficult. Some pupils find it helpful to underline key words in the questions to help them to focus on what is being looked for. In this question, the key word is 'changed'. So you know that you are looking for information about the American Diet **changing** between 1950 and 1970. You will gain only one mark for making a point about the American diet in 1950 and only one mark for making a point about the change in the American diet by 1970. You need to make **both** points to gain two marks.

   (b) McDonalds (1)
        'one company more than any other '(1)

2. The story of how McDonald's started gives only the company's version of what happened, which the author distrusts (2).
    OR
    The writer does not believe/is suspicious of the story told by McDonald's about how it started (2).
    OR
    The story McDonald's tells about how it started may not be the truth – the writer is doubtful about the official company story (2).

TOP EXAM TIP

This question asks you about the writer's attitude or opinion towards the subject he is writing about. You can work out the writer's attitude or opinion from the words and ideas the writer uses. The word 'conveyed' means 'communicated' or 'told'. Did you work out that the writer might feel distrustful or suspicious about what the company has said about itself? You will gain **one** mark for making the point that there is a McDonald's 'version' of how the company started. Your **second** mark is for explaining how the writer feels about this.

3. He was a salesman for Multimixers and wondered why the hamburger stand needed so many Multimixers (2).
    OR
    He was surprised by how many/the large number of Multimixers the stand used (2).

TOP EXAM TIP

This is what we call an 'understanding' question – these ask you to explain ideas or information in the passage. Question 1 was also an 'understanding' question.

4. The food was tasty (1).
    AND/OR
    The fries were crisp (1).
    AND/OR
    The milkshakes were thick (1).

TOP EXAM TIP

Some pupils find it helpful to underline key words in the questions to help them to focus on what is being looked for. In this question, the key word is 'popular'. Did you find this word in the third sentence of paragraph two? This time, the answer comes BEFORE the key word 'popular'. Remember that the answer can come before or after a key word or phrase so look <u>around</u> for the answer.

You gain one mark for each reason you give for why McDonald's was popular – up to a maximum of two marks. There are three suggestions here but in your answer you only need to give two reasons to gain two marks.

5. Most men of his age would not want to start a new business/would want to retire/work less hard (1) and would not want to start a business/build a new company (1)

HINT

You will often be asked about an idea in the passage but you have to answer 'in your own words'. Many pupils answer these questions by quoting the exact words from the passage. You will not be given any marks for doing this! For example, if you had written for this answer 'slowing down' without explaining what it means you would be given no marks as you have simply copied this phrase from the passage.

6. (a) 'rinky-dink' = poor quality/amateurish/not efficient or professional (2)
    (b) 'streamlined' (2)
        OR
        'efficient' (2)

HINT

Did you notice that you can gain either two marks or 0 marks for your answers here? You are given two marks here if you get the answer right as Question 6A and 6B are quite difficult questions!

7. (a) They were on the cover of a magazine (1)
    (b) People visited often to see why the business was so successful (1)

TOP EXAM TIP

Did you spot the word 'legendary' in the first sentence of paragraph 2? 'Legendary' means famous and examples of this are written in the next sentence.

In question 4, you were asked to explain **in your own words** so there was no need to quote. And sometimes you are asked to **quote** so there is no need to use your own words. In question 7, you are not told to answer in your own words. So it is OK to use your own words OR quote.

If you are ever not sure whether to quote or use your own words, do both!

8. He might want to take the credit/he wanted people to think he had discovered or invented McDonalds/he was the reason for its success (2).

TOP EXAM TIP

This question asks for your opinion – the key phrase in the question is 'Why do you think...'.

Of course, your answer must be based on your understanding of the passage – as well as your general knowledge. In this case, you can work out from the passage that McDonalds was very successful and so you could guess that Ray Kroc might want to think this was all down to him.

9. (a) 'Metaphor' OR 'imagery' (1). It tells you that they announced/told/stated the numbers loudly (1).

    (b) They put up signs (1) saying how many they sold (1).

TOP EXAM TIP

This is an 'analysis' question which asks you about the writer's word choice. Did you spot that 'trumpeted' is a metaphor? Sometimes you will be told that you are analysing a metaphor or simile but – more likely – you will be asked to identify the technique just as you are in this question. Of course, you have to notice that this is an image and you should also know what type of image it is - a metaphor!

10. 1952: First franchise in Phoenix (1)

    1954: Ray Kroc arrived (1)

TOP EXAM TIP

In this question, the examiner helps you by telling you where to look for the answer! Just find the date 1952 and work out what happened then – the answer comes before the date. Then you are told that this was 'two years before' Ray Kroc arrived.

11. 'true heroes' (1)

    'remarkable men' (1)

12. (a) Customers would come to a window (1) rather than having items brought to the car (1).

    (b) They made the menu smaller/they put only seven things on the menu/they 'cut the menu to just seven items' (1).

    AND/OR

    They decided/chose what to give customers instead of customers deciding (1).

    AND/OR

    The burgers were smaller and cheaper (1).

    (c) 'novel' or 'entirely novel' ('new' = no marks) (2)

13. Dashes are used to show that this phrase explains in more detail/adds extra information about the hamburger size (2)

TOP EXAM TIP

This is an 'analysis' question. In other words, you are being asked about the language the writer has used – HOW the writer writes. Any question that asks you about punctuation is an 'analysis' question.

HINT

You can learn how to answer 'punctuation' questions quite easily by knowing about the uses of various punctuation marks – here are some examples.

Commas – to separate items in a list, clarify sentences that could be misleading and/or used in direct speech

Semi-colon – to join two or more closely related ideas and/or to separate sets of items in a list when there are commas within the sets or lists

Colon or dash – to introduce a list or quotations and/or expand on the meaning of a previous idea

Two dashes – to separate out a phrase or clause or comment

Brackets – to separate a piece of additional information

14. The word 'flop' is informal/slang (1). It means the change was a complete/utter failure. (1)

TOP EXAM TIP

This is another 'analysis' question which asks you to think about the writer's craft. You are being asked about the words the writer has chosen to use.

When answering analysis questions, many pupils fall into the trap of explaining WHAT the sentence means. Of course, this sentence tells you that the change was not successful or was a failure or did not appeal to people. But the question asks you what is unusual or interesting about the word 'flop'– not what it means!

The question also asks you to say if the word choice is effective – it is effective because 'flop' does not just mean 'failure' but 'utter and complete failure'. This makes clear to us that the change was completely unsuccessful.

15. They appealed to families (1)
because they sold items for children such as fries and milkshakes (1).
OR
because the food tasted great (1).
OR
because it was cheap to feed a whole family (1).

TOP EXAM TIP

Did you know that 'clientele' means 'customers'? If so, then this question is straightforward as the word 'family' comes straight after it. Try to keep building your vocabulary in the run up to the exam by reading as much as possible and learning the meanings of any unfamiliar words – a large vocabulary will help you in the exam.

16. They invented machines and systems such as dispensers (1).
AND/OR
They introduced 'specialisation' where one person does one task (1).
AND/OR
Food was ready prepared so customers did not have to wait (1).

17. (a) I think McDonald's customers enjoyed eating at McDonald's (1)
because they could collect their food from a window (1).
AND/OR
because the food was cheap and arrived quickly (1).
AND/OR
because you would have the same experience every time (1).

TOP EXAM TIP

You gain one mark for your opinion – either writing you think customers would enjoy eating at McDonald's or that they would not enjoy eating at McDonald's. There is no right or wrong answer here because this is your own opinion. Then you have to find reasons for your opinion from the passage to gain the second mark. There are three examples of reasons given above – you gain one mark for one reason.

(b) I think McDonald's employees enjoyed working at McDonald's. (1) They did not have to serve customers in their cars and they could concentrate on one task at a time (1).
OR
They used machines which made their jobs easier (1).
OR
They could prepare the food in advance (1).
OR
They only had to serve a small number of items (1).

TOP EXAM TIP

You gain one mark for your opinion – either writing you think employees would enjoy working at McDonald's or that they would not enjoy working at McDonald's. There is no right or wrong answer here because this is your own opinion. Then you have to find reasons for this from the passage. There are lots of examples of reasons given above.

18. C because Bill Bryson uses many facts and figures OR statistics about how it started OR who started it and what it sells. (2)

HINT   In question 18, you will gain one mark for identifying the purpose correctly and one mark for giving a clearly explained reason for your answer.

TOP EXAM TIP

You may be asked about purpose at General level. Think about why the writer has written the passage. Writers write texts for many different purposes. Look at the list of purposes below, and remember that a writer usually has more than one purpose.

- To entertain
- To persuade
- To explain
- To inform
- To argue
- To evaluate

19. The title is appropriate (1) because
    It contains information about McDonald's in the 1950s (1).
    OR
    It describes the development of McDonald's from 1950 onwards (1).
    OR
    It is about developments in technology (1).

    ## TOP EXAM TIP

    You are asked here for your opinion. You might think the title is not appropriate – as long as you give a clear, well-explained reason, you will get the marks. One mark is awarded for giving your opinion and the second mark is awarded for giving a reason for your opinion.

INTRODUCTION

This section gives you advice about the Standard Grade English Writing exam. The first part gives you general help with how to write in the exam. The second part gives you specific advice about how to tackle each writing option.

As well as advice, you will find.

> ### TOP EXAM TIP
> These are 'at a glance' tasks to do or advice to remember

All pupils – whether working at Credit, General or Foundation level – sit the same Writing paper. The Writing paper is in booklet form and contains anything between 20 and 25 questions/essay titles. There are also pictures and photographs on the left hand side pages of the booklet. In the exam, you will choose ONE of the questions/ essay titles.

You are given 75 minutes for this exam. You should always spend some of this time planning what you are going to write. Take your time at this stage – it is better to spend 10 minutes calmly choosing and planning your writing than to start writing in a hurry, change your mind and have to start all over again!

Give yourself an hour for the actual writing itself – how many words can you write in an hour? If you do not know, you should find this out. We all write at different speeds so you can only find this out on your own. Your friends could be very fast or very slow writers so don't compare yourself with them. Work out how much you can write and aim to be able to do this in the exam itself.

If you often run out of time, practice will help. For example, you may be trying to write stories that are simply too long – perhaps because you do not spend time on planning the plot/storyline and so try to cover too much in the story itself. Practise planning and writing simpler shorter stories – fewer characters or fewer events perhaps – and this may help you to finish on time.

Always leave 5 minutes at the end for a final read through. Even if you have not finished your writing, try to take time for a check. Spelling and punctuation errors can spoil the overall effect of a piece of writing so take the time to ensure your sentences make sense.

> ### TOP EXAM TIP
> Every year, a number of pupils do not follow the instructions at the beginning of the paper which tell you to choose ONE question from the paper.
>
> There are usually between 20 and 25 questions to choose from. Choose ONE only!

Preparation before the big day!

Lots of people will tell you that you can't prepare for the English Writing paper. The truth is that you <u>can</u> prepare for the Writing paper and the more preparation you do, the better your writing will be.

The best preparation is to write, write, write! Whether it is letters or emails to your friends, stories, your diary or writing for other subjects like History, all writing practice will be useful when it comes to the exam. Of course, you will not know exactly what Writing questions will be in the exam paper but you can practise by looking at past papers – or working through some examples from the Writing Paper in this book – because the same types of writing almost always appear in the exam. For example, there are usually questions that ask you to write short stories, to write about personal experience, descriptive writing and so on. So looking at practice papers will give you a very good idea of what to expect.

> ### TOP EXAM TIP
>
> The proper term for a type of writing is 'genre'. How many genres are there in English? Challenge yourself to see how many you can come up with!

Using pictures/photographs

Another good way to prepare for the exam is to look at photographs or pictures and use these pictures to help your writing. There are always pictures and/or photos in the Writing exam paper so this will be good practice for the exam day itself. Don't ignore the pictures in the paper. A photo or picture is there to help you. It can give you ideas and inspiration. Really look at the picture in detail and think of words and ideas as you examine it. For example, you might be shown a photo of a dark, gloomy forest and one of the tasks is to write an atmospheric piece of descriptive writing. As you look closely at the picture, you may think of words like 'frightening', 'secretive', 'silent'. You may even see a dim ruined castle in a corner of the picture and this might spark off an idea – perhaps you could include a description of the castle as well as the forest? Let your imagination run wild … Don't worry if you find it challenging to use pictures for inspiration – you do not have to use ideas from the photo or picture at all if you do not want to. And there are always questions at the end of the paper without any pictures.

Choosing a genre

Another good idea is to practise more than one type of writing. You may love writing short stories and so you may have decided to write one in the exam. But what if the short story questions in the exam do not appeal to you? Practise writing at least TWO genres to prepare for the exam. For example, you may enjoy writing informative pieces such as news articles or reports but you could also practise your personal writing so you have more questions to choose from in the exam.

> ### TOP EXAM TIP
>
> Don't forget about spelling, punctuation and paragraphing. A good way to work on these aspects is to get someone – a teacher, a friend, your parent/carer – to look over your work. Get into the habit of reading over your work by reading it out loud, in your head or to friends or family to make sure your writing makes sense.

On examination day

Firstly, punctuation, spelling and grammar. These are sometimes called the 'technical' aspects of English. All your sentences must make sense clearly 'at first reading'. This means the examiner should not have to re-read a sentence because the meaning is unclear. Place commas in the right places especially when you are writing complex sentences. Do try to write as accurately as you can. Checking over your work by reading it to yourself can help to ensure your sentences make sense. If it doesn't make sense to you, it won't make sense to the examiner!

Now, length. Pupils often ask how long an essay written in an exam has to be. The simple answer is that there is no limit because we all write at different speeds and we all write different amounts. Also, think about your purpose. You might choose to write 'in any way' about a given title and you choose to write a poem. A poem of, say, 600–700 words would be very long indeed! This is what is meant by the phrase 'appropriate to purpose'. The length should 'fit' the purpose – and of course is also related to the amount of time you have in the exam.

Let's think some more about this idea of purpose. You must be very clear about the purpose of the writing task you choose. For example, you might choose to write a short story. One of the main purposes of a short story is to entertain the reader. So your story has to be entertaining! If your purpose is to create a gently humorous story that will make the reader laugh, then it must communicate this gentle humour. Otherwise, it won't 'fulfil its purpose'. Never change purpose in the middle of a piece of writing – if you start writing a short story about a character in a dilemma, don't get carried away so much that this turns into a personal story about a time when you were in a dilemma. You can, of course, think about your own experience and even use some of these details, but you must stick to the purpose in the question.

Words, words, words ...

What about the actual words you use? When writing, pupils can sometimes be so busy with character, setting, ideas, organisation and all the rest that they forget about the actual words they are using! Try to use language in interesting and original ways – not just as words to tell a story or explain an experience or express an opinion.

You could use:

- imagery such as similes and metaphors
- interesting sentence structures – different sentence lengths and patterns
- language to create a mood or atmosphere, for example to build up tension in a ghost story

Have a look at the Practice Close Reading passages. The writers of these passages have all used interesting and original language.

PERSONAL WRITING

> 1. Write about a journey or trip you have made. Remember to include your thoughts and feelings.
> 4. Write about your experience of a new baby in the family. Remember to include your thoughts and feelings.
> 8. Write about your hopes and dreams for the future.
> 15. Write about the music you enjoy and what it means to you.
> 21. 'It wasn't us!' Write about an experience you have had where you were part of a group blamed for something.

These questions are all examples of Personal Writing. The important thing to remember – whether you are writing about something that has already happened (for example, question 1) or about things which might happen in the future (for example, question 10) – is to write 'from the heart'. The best Personal Writing is truthful and open and describes your feelings and emotions clearly. For example, if you do not play tennis, it would be difficult to pretend you know all about tennis and to write honestly about how it makes you feel.

Remember also that Personal Writing should include description of sights, sounds, surroundings, atmosphere – if you do not include this kind of description, your writing will end up being a list of events and nothing else. Try to make your writing lively and not just 'Then we did this', or 'Then I did that'! This is one reason why the question usually reminds you to include your 'thoughts and feelings'.

> *Can you spot the differences between the two extracts below?*
>
> *We got up at 5 o'clock in the morning. We were very tired. We packed our cases and waited for the taxi. The taxi arrived and we went to the airport.*
>
> *We got up at 5 o'clock in the morning and looked out of the frosty icy window. We were very tired but so excited to be heading off towards heat and sunshine! We packed our cases, the two of us sitting on them to make sure they closed. They sprang open every time we tried to stuff in another last minute 'essential'. The taxi arrived promptly at 6 o'clock and whisked us off to the airport.*

This type of writing is about your emotions. It is about reflecting on how you felt or feel about something or someone. When you are writing about an experience, you should explain how you felt before, during and after the experience. For example, if you choose Question 21, describe your feelings/emotions:
- before the event (before you were blamed)
- at the time of/during the event (the moment when you were blamed)
- afterwards (when the true culprit was found).

This is called 'chronological order' – in other words, write about the events you are describing in the order that they happened. So, if you choose question 5 about a new baby in the family, you could use the chronological order below:

- When/how I found out mum was expecting
- My feelings when I found out
- First six months – mum very well, my exams!
- Last three months – mum in hospital, baby early
- Birth – what happened/my feelings
- How I feel now baby is 12 months old

It is more difficult to choose a structure if you are writing questions 4, 8 or 15. This is because these ask you about the future or about something which is not a 'one-off' event. Your essay should have a clear structure so think about how you will organise your writing. For example, in question 15, you could use the structure below:

- Introduction
- How/when/why I started playing the trumpet
- My band
- How I have improved – my teacher/practice
- Competitions/prizes I have won
- My dreams of playing at the Albert Hall

In question 10, you will have to think about how you want to organise your writing. Perhaps you could divide your hopes and dreams into different areas – your career ambitions, your hopes about your family, your interests, your dream of becoming rich and famous! So your writing will have four main sections.

Some pupils find mind maps helpful to organise their writing. Here is a mind map of the ideas for question 10:

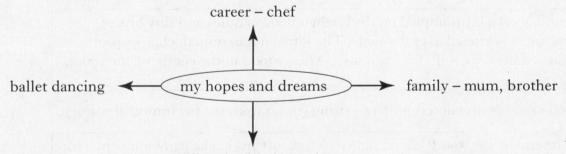

For question 4, how about writing first about where you want to be, your goal? Then write about the different ways you are going to reach or have reached this goal, finishing off with the importance of achieving your goal at the end?

Remember that you can organise your Personal Writing in any way that 'fits' with what you are writing about – as long as it is organised!

Personal Writing is a very popular choice for many pupils. It is a chance to write about yourself and about something that has happened to you so, because everyone is different no-one will be able to write exactly the same as you. A lot of pupils choose this option so try to make your writing stand out. If you follow the advice above, you will be well on the way to writing success.

SHORT STORY

2. Write a short story about a character who makes a train journey. You should develop setting, character and plot.

7. Write a short story using the following opening
    He emerged from the time machine and looked out over a strange crystal city he did not recognise. The buildings shone brightly but there was no movement. No life.

12. Write a short story about a sporting champion who loses a match/game at a crucial time. You should develop setting, character and plot.

14. Write a short story about a busker. You should develop setting, character and plot.

20 Write a short story in which the main character makes a life-changing decision. You should develop setting and character as well as plot.

Usually, a 'short story' question will help you with what you need to do – you will be told 'You should develop setting and character as well as plot'. So that is exactly what you should do!

Many pupils write short stories that have lots of action happening (the 'plot' or 'storyline') but they forget to develop the setting of the story or the character(s).

Setting

TOP EXAM TIP

Describe the setting – both time and place. This can be done in 'chunks', for example, in a paragraph(s) near the beginning of your writing and/or can be 'spread' throughout your writing.

Here is an example of description of setting (place) from the beginning of a story:

The birthday cake lay trampled on the kitchen floor, candles and tiny bits of icing and sugar scattered over the table. The kitchen was ruined, chairs upset and cutlery, plates, cups all dirty and torn. Missy stood in the centre of the room, sobbing quietly.

Here is an example of a description of setting (time) from the beginning of a story:

It was the end of the war. Richard sighed as took off his khaki army uniform with its tight jacket and brass buttons and counted out his few remaining shillings. Time to go home.

Can you spot 'clues' to where and when these stories take place?

Characters

One very common mistake pupils make is to assume that the reader knows all about a character. Remember that although you may feel you know a character, you need to describe him or her to the reader by using plenty of detail.

So make sure you develop your character(s) – ask yourself:

- How does she/he change, develop, grow?
- How does he/she behave and speak?
- What does he/she look like?
- How does he/she relate to other people?
- What are his/her opinions/point of view?

Show what characters are like through the way they speak, act and through their relationships.

Theme

What will the theme of your story be? Sometimes, the question will tell you this – for example, in Question 20, you are told that a 'life change' will be the theme of this story – but how will you develop this theme? Will the life change be a positive decision for all the characters? What are the results of the life change? How will the story end? Will your story have a moral or message such as 'Don't cry over spilt milk'?

TOP EXAM TIP

Popular themes include:

- Relationships
- Conflict
- Love
- Good versus evil
- Freedom

Can you think of any others you would like to write about?

Whatever grade you are aiming to achieve, you will have to organise your story. It needs to have a beginning, a middle and an end. Usually, a story will build towards a climax towards the end of the story. For example, if you are answering question 20, the 'life-changing decision' could happen about two-thirds of the way through the story – after you have built up your plot and developed your characters. After your character makes the decision, you could write about the effects of this.

You can use techniques such as flashbacks to create a more interesting structure. The important thing is to plan out the structure before you start. That way, your story won't 'ramble' and the reader will be able to follow the plot clearly.

Short stories are always very popular with pupils – so try to make yours stand out from the crowd.

DISCURSIVE WRITING

5. Over 9000 babies are born each year in Scotland to mothers aged between 13 and 19. Give your views.

9. Mobile phones – a nuisance or an essential piece of technology? Give your views.

13. The Scottish Government wants to encourage school pupils to be healthy, for example, by providing healthy school dinners and encouraging pupils to take PE. Give your views.

16. 'Pop is actually my least favourite kind of music because it lacks real depth.' (Christina Aguilera) Give your views.

17. Zoos are cruel and inhumane. Give your views.

This type of writing should not be attempted unless you have thought about the subject before the exam! If you have never reflected on zoos and zoo conditions, have never visited a zoo and don't really like animals, you are not going to write a convincing essay about why you think such places are cruel.

You should try to include facts and information in Discursive Writing and you will only have these if you have read or thought about the topic in advance. For example, if you are writing about mobile phones, do you know how many people own a mobile phone, statistics about mobile phone companies, information about the alleged dangers to your health of using mobile phones? Background knowledge always improves Discursive Writing because it shows you are knowledgeable about the topic and have already thought about it.

If you choose to write a Discursive essay, you should be very organised because a clear structure is a requirement of this type of writing.

The first thing to do is to decide what you think about the topic. Do you agree, disagree or can you 'see' both sides of the argument? You should state your opinion about this clearly at the beginning of your essay. This will be your introductory paragraph.

You should then explain the arguments for or against (or both) in the main body of the essay. The way to organise this clearly is to use topic sentences. A topic sentence is usually the first sentence in a paragraph, although it can actually occur anywhere in the paragraph. (Why not try experimenting with writing a paragraph and placing the topic sentences in different places within the paragraph?) The topic sentence explains the main point you make in the paragraph, for example, you think zoos are cruel because all the animals are caged or locked in. Remember that you should include information and examples in each paragraph too.

Your conclusion should repeat your opinion clearly and 'finish off' your essay strongly.

TOP EXAM TIP

It's important to stick to your opinion – don't change your mind halfway through! You either agree, disagree or you can understand both sides. Make sure the end of your essay 'matches' the beginning.

There is a lot of advice about Discursive Writing in Leckie & Leckie's *Standard Grade Revision Notes*. Have a look at this for plenty of useful advice: see www.leckieandleckie.co.uk

WRITING IN A SPECIFIC FORMAT

Questions 3 and 11 ask you to write a letter. If you choose this question, you must be familiar with the correct layout for a letter – in both questions, you are being asked to write a formal letter.

Can you remember all the rules about the layout and language in this type of letter?

* Where should your address should go?
* Where should you add the date?
* Should you include the address you are writing to?
* How should you start the letter?
* What do you call the person you are writing to?
* Should you use paragraphs?
* How do you finish off the letter?

If you are unclear about this, give this question a miss!

Letters also need to have a clear structure – look at the suggested structure below for a letter of complaint:

Introduction – state clearly the issue you wish to write/complain about.

      Explain your opinion about it.

      Give some facts and figures which support your opinion.

Middle section – explain in more detail about the problem.

      Give examples of what this means/has meant for you/your community.

Conclusion – restate your opinion.

      Explain what you want to be done about the situation. (For example, you could make positive suggestions about alternatives.)

There are occasionally questions that ask you to write in other formats, for example, a newspaper article or a speech or a diary or a play script. There is not enough space here for advice on all these types. However, you should attempt this type of question only if you are very familiar with the format, layout and language that you should use.

DESCRIPTIVE WRITING

> 19. Describe the scene brought to mind by one of the following:
>
> 'A full moon hangs, a round, white blaze.'
>
> OR
>
> 'Bare branches in winter are a form of writing.'

This is one of the most challenging types of writing – but if you are a confident writer with a very well – developed vocabulary, it could be the one for you.

- Do you love using imagery and description using plenty of adjectives in original ways?
- Are you able to describe a person, an object, a landscape for longer than a few paragraphs?
- Are you able to organise your descriptive writing? For example, you might decide to describe each aspect of the scene in turn and so you will have to decide on an order for this.

TOP EXAM TIP

Try to appeal to all five senses in descriptive writing – not just what you can see in the scene.

- What can be heard?
- What textures are there?
- What can be touched or felt?
- What can be smelt?
- What can be tasted?

You don't have to describe all five senses but even using one or two will make your writing livelier and more interesting.

Think about how to narrate your writing –

'I watch the moon slip down...'

OR

'The moon slips down...'

Which do you prefer?

If you enjoy Descriptive Writing, it can be tempting to write randomly all sorts of great descriptive words and phrases just as they come to you! But a descriptive essay needs to have some kind of logical order so that the reader can follow it clearly.

Could you:

- use the five senses as five 'sections' in your essay?
- describe each aspect of the scene in turn, e.g. trees, branches, twigs, sky?
- describe the scene from different places, e.g. as though you are moving through the scene, e.g. watching the moon from ground level, halfway up a hill, at the top of the hill?

TOP EXAM TIP

To improve your descriptive writing, look at photographs or pictures and practise describing these in as much detail as you can.

Remember that you have 75 minutes to write in the exam so you need to include as much detail as possible.

WRITE IN ANY WAY...

6. ' Bringing Up Baby.' Write in any way you like using this title
10. Write in any way you like about the picture above.
18. You've got a friend.' Write in any way you like about friendship.

These questions are great if you do not find a question in the paper that 'springs out' at you – or if you are good at lots of types of writing. These questions give you freedom to choose what genre you want to write. You could write a poem, a drama script, a fictional diary... just remember that you have to be confident and experienced in writing the genre you choose.

Of course, all the usual rules apply – planning your writing, organising it well with a clear structure, expressing yourself clearly and well – whatever you write.

Most importantly, enjoy yourself! There is lots to think about when you are creating a piece of writing, especially under exam pressure, but try to relax and enjoy the opportunity to let your imagination run free!